TABLE OF CONTENTS

Part 1

Part 2

Part 3

Part 4

The GIRL WITHOUT a FACE

tearontaron

PART 1

Me and My Girlfriend

I'VE GOT MYSELF ...
...A GIRL-FRIEND.

HER BLACK, BRAIDED HAIR...

...PALE SKIN...

...AND LITTLE MOLES HERE AND THERE...

...ARE SOME OF HER MANY CHARMING FEATURES.

I'M HOME.
!
BUT HER MOST DEFINING FEATURE WOULD HAVE TO BE...

...HER LACK OF A FACE.

BY A STRANGE TURN OF EVENTS ...

...I STARTED A JOB IN ZABO TOWN...
YOU COOKED UP SOME JUMBO PORTIONS TODAY!
... HALF A YEAR AGO.
座坊町コーポ

SIGN: ZABO TOWN APARTMENTS

......
?

SHE'S A QUIET ONE.

SO THERE ARE PLENTY OF MOMENTS WHEN I CAN'T GET A READ ON WHAT SHE'S THINKING.
?
SOMETHING ON MY FACE?

WELL... WHAT IS IT, THEN?
WRONG
WRONG

LOOK THERE.

?
OUTSIDE ?

SAME OLD SCENERY.

WHAT'S UP—

......
......

OH.
I GET IT...
LIKE...A WELCOME-HOME KISS?
EVERY DAY WITH HER...
...IS FULL OF LITTLE MYSTERIES.
MHM!
MHM!

BUT WHAT'S NOT A MYSTERY ...
...IS HER LOVE FOR ME.

Bonus: First Time Getting Dolled Up

SOWA (FIDGET)
そわ
SOWA
そわ
DON'T BE NERVOUS, HON.

Her on the Way Home

NOT TO BRAG, BUT I'VE GOT A GIRL-FRIEND.

THE THING IS...
...SHE'S GOT NO FACE.

Za-bo Town.
Zabo Town.
PUSHUUU (FSSHH)
HAVEN'T SEEN YOU IN A WHILE.
YEAH, I WAS AWAY FOR BUSINESS.
THAT SO? SUCH A HARD WORKER.
ZABO TOWN BUS

YOU TAKE CARE OF YOURSELF, OKAY!?
WILL DO.

ERM...... YOU WANT CUCUMBERS AND TOMATOES? TWO EACH?

SORRY, I CAN'T UNDERSTAND YOU THE WAY THAT MAN OF YOURS CAN.
BUT HERE YA GO.

BECAUSE SHE'S A QUIET PERSON...
......

...AND BECAUSE OTHERS CAN'T READ HER FACE...

...IT SEEMS COMMUNI-CATION CAN BE TRICKY SOME-TIMES.

ばっ!!
BA (FWIP)
I'M BACK!
!

......

......

I WAS THINKING OF RUNNING HOME AND HIDING...

KAAAAA (BLUUUUSH)

...BUT SURPRISING YOU THIS WAY WAS JUST AS GOOD.

WELL? DID I SURPRI—
URK!?

WHOA THERE! SH-SHEESH! THAT HURTS!
WHOAAA...
KORO (ROLL)
SURI (GRIND)
SURI
SURI
SURI
KORO
C'MON! COOL IT!

GLAD TO BE HOME, THOUGH.
SHE CAN'T SPEAK OR SHOW EXPRES-SIONS, BUT...

...WHEN THE MESSAGE IS "HAPPY YOU'RE HOME"...
...I RECEIVE IT LOUD AND CLEAR.

Always Thinking of You

LOOKS PERFECT ON YOU!
HAIRPIN I PURCHASED WHILE ON BUSINESS TRIP

Her and the Wall-Slam

BOOK: MASQUERADE HEAVEN

SFX: POI (TOSS)

BECAUSE SHE DOESN'T HAVE FACIAL EXPRESSIONS...
I THINK I LOVE YA, BABE...
I...

...
...AND IS SO QUIET AND COMPOSED ...

W......
WELL? WHADDAYA THINK......?
かあああああぁ...
KAAAAAAA (BLUUUUUUSH)
...EVERY DAY IS FULL OF MYSTERIES.

H-HEART POUNDING YET...?
......

I WAS HOPING FOR A REACTION OF SOME KIND......
......

S-SURE. NOT FOR EVERYONE, I GUESS ...

MAYBE... IT IS A LITTLE CHILDISH AFTER ALL...
......

BO (FLUSH)

I WAS SURE GIRLS LOVED THIS KINDA STUFF, BUT......

MAYBE YOU'D BE INTO MORE-REALISTIC STUFF......
LIKE TV DRAMAS...
WOWWWW!
WORKED LIKE A CHARM

AH! HANG ON—CHECK OUT THIS LOVEY-DOVEY SCENE...
BA (SPIN)
...!?

HUH...? IS SHE... IN A BAD MOOD NOW?

SFX: TSUUUN (HMPH)

The Whole Truth...

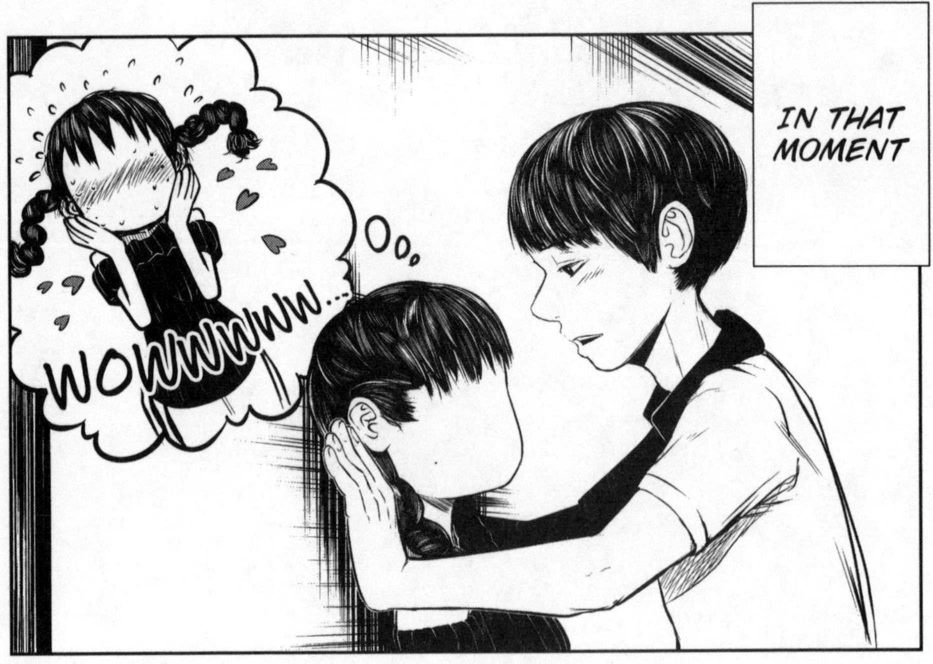
IN THAT MOMENT
WOWWWWWW...
Ooo

Her and Memories

MOMI
モミ
MOMI (KNEAD)
モミ
MOMI
モミ
AHHH...
AMAZING! YOU'RE GREAT AT THIS!
NOT TO BRAG, BUT I'VE GOT A GIRLFRIEND.

ALL RIGHT, LET'S SWITCH.
I'LL GIVE THE BACK RUB NOW.
!
THANKS.
...

THE THING IS, SHE'S GOT NO FACE.
......
じー...
JIII (STAAARE)
? WHAT'S WRONG?

CHON (POKE)
ちょん
ちょん CHON
OH. THAT.
YEAH, THAT SCAR'S FROM WHEN I WAS LITTLE. GOT INTO A FIGHT...
... WITH A FRIEND.

SINCE SHE'S SO QUIET BY NATURE, EVERY DAY...
ZABO MART
...IS FULL OF MYSTERIES.

TON
TON (TAP)
ALREADY LOOKS LIKE A TROUBLEMAKER, RIGHT? SHE LIVED IN MY NEIGHBORHOOD.

ALBUM
DOSA (THUD)
HERE WE GO! MY OLD PHOTO ALBUMS!

HMM? HMM?
AH! THERE— SHE'S THE ONE!

CAN'T EVEN RECALL WHAT STARTED IT...
...BUT YEAH, WE GOT INTO A FIGHT, AND, WELL......
IT BLEW OVER SOON ENOUGH, THOUGH ...
...AND WE WERE RIGHT BACK TO BEING PALS.

ALL THE WAY THROUGH HIGH SCHOOL.
MAN, THIS BRINGS BACK MEMORIES...

WE WERE SUCH GOOD FRIENDS ...
...

CONGRATS! GRADUATION
SURI (RUB)
SURI
I WONDER... WHAT SHE'S UP TO THESE DAYS.
...

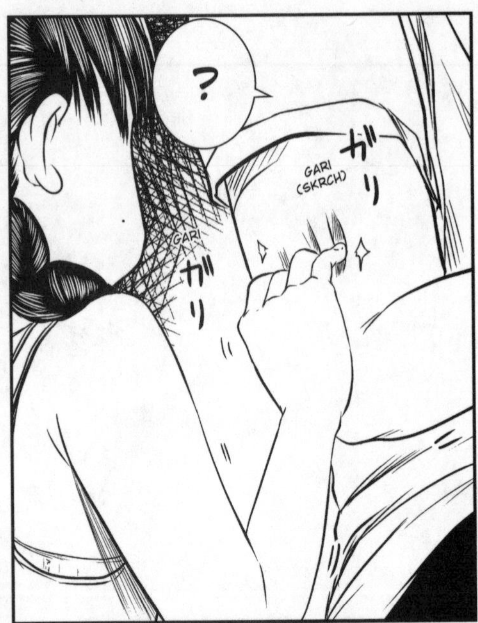
?
ガリ
GARI (SKRCH)
GARI
ガリ

?? I'M, UH, NOT ITCHY.
KARI
カリ
KARI
カリ
KARI
カリ
KARI
カリカリカリ…
KARI
KARI
カリ
KARI
カリ
KARI
HEY, THAT HURTS.
WHAT'S UP?

……
SAWA
さわ
SAWA
さわ
さわ
SAWA (RUB)

SHUN (GLOOM)
しゅん…
パタン
PATAN (FWUP)

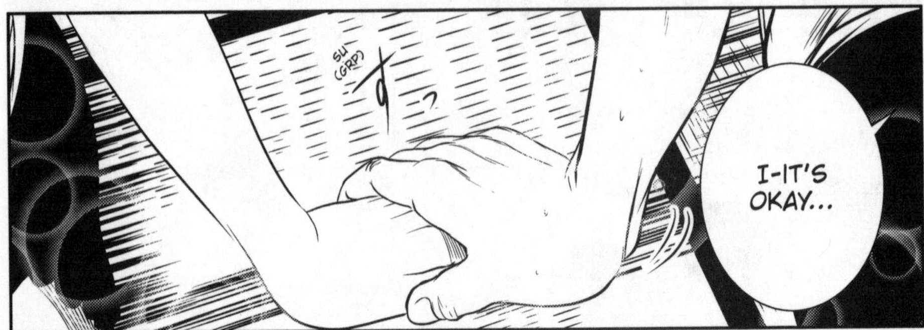
SU (GRP)
す
I-IT'S OKAY…

REALLY, DON'T WORRY. I'M IN THIS WITH YOU FOR THE LONG HAUL!
YOU'RE LEAVING PLENTY OF SCARS ON MY HEART. IN A GOOD WAY, I MEAN...
...EVERY DAY IS FULL OF MYSTERIES—
BECAUSE MY GIRLFRIEND HAS NO FACE...
......SORRY, WAS MY SUAVE ACT TOO MUCH? OVERLY CHEESY? HA-HA-HA-HA.........
♪

IT'S FINE, IT'S FINE!
NADE なで
NADE NADE (RUB) なで
BUT SHE MAKES HERSELF REALLY CLEAR SOMETIMES...
JUST IN CASE YOU NEED TO HEAR IT AGAIN...
...I'M YOURS NOW AND FOREVER. ♡
ペコリ PEKORI (BOW)
...AND THAT JEALOUS SIDE IS CUTE AS HECK.

I Want to Scar You Too

YER STILL LOOKING AT THESE PHOTOS?
♡
1 MONTH OLD–8/6/1984
NADE
なで
?
NADE
なで
LET ME LEAVE MY MARK ON THAT HEART...

Her and Intimacy

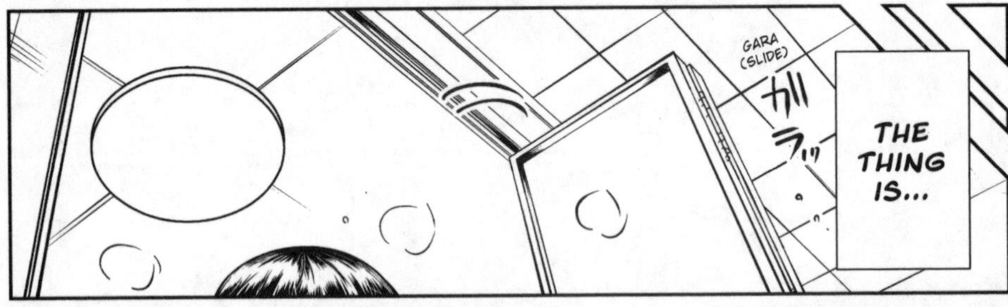

LOST MORE WEIGHT THAN EXPECTED

...AND SHE TENDS TO BE ON THE QUIETER SIDE, EVERY DAY...
ずんっ
ZUN (FWMP)
!

......? BEING KINDA PLAYFUL TODAY...
SFX: URI (WOBBLE) URI

NOT EXACTLY SURE WHY......
WISH I COULD GET A GAL.
SAME. FOR REAL.
...IS FULL OF MYS-TERIES.
CLUB ZABO

WHOA, CAREFUL THERE.
URI
URI

WHAT'S GOING ON?
KORON (FLIP) コロン
POFU (PWOOF) ぽふっ

AH! HMM? IS IT...
OH!?

...NEW LAUNDRY DETERGENT? YOU SMELL A LITTLE DIFFERENT ......
FURU
FURU (SHAKE)

HMM...
THIS ISN'T WORKING ...

CAN'T SEE THE TV THIS WAY...
...
ZUN (FWUMP)

OH!

YOU HAVE A MOLE ON YOUR HEAD. NEVER KNEW IT WAS THERE BEFORE.
...

SHUN (GLOOM)
HMM. WHAT COULD IT BE? ALL THIS TOUCHY-FEELINESS ......
BEING ALL CLINGY... HMM? ...HANG ON? ...THAT REMINDS ME...

Sudden clinginess from your partner? Be warned !!
• It could be a sign they don't trust you!!
Are you letting your partner know you love them enough? A sudden increase in attempts at physical intimacy could be their way of trying to confirm your feelings for them!
HEH. NO WORRIES ABOUT THAT WITH US.

BA (CHUP)
DON'T WORRY, BABE!!
!?

NO NEED TO FRET!! YOU'RE...... THE ONLY ONE FOR ME!!
!?
BECAUSE I LOVE YOU!!
AND I'M NOT GOING ANYWHERE!
SO REST EASY!!
WOWWWW...
うひゃ
あああぁぁ.
YES, WHEN YOUR GIRLFRIEND HAS NO FACE, EVERY DAY...
WH-WHAT'S WRONG!?
EEEEE.♡
...IS FULL OF MYS-TERIES.

O-OH WOW! JUST WOW!
YOU'VE REALLY BEEN WORKING OUT! YOU'RE SO AMAZING!
KOKU
KOKU (NOD)
EVERYTHING I SAID EARLIER WAS ALSO TRUE, OF COURSE......
TIME TO DIET!!

Her and a Day Out

NOT TO BRAG, BUT I'VE GOT A GIRLFRIEND.
KOKU (NOD)
ANOTHER SCORCHER TODAY, HUH?

THE THING IS, SHE'S GOT...
PATA (FLAP)
PATA
...NO FACE.
MIIN (KREEE)
MIIN
MIIN

LET'S PICK UP WHAT WE NEED FOR DINNER ON THE WAY HOME?
KOKU
KOKU
HOT AS HELL...

KAAA (CAW)
KAAA

GASA (RUSTLE)
GASA
WE REALLY LOADED UP, HUH?

SOWA
そわ
そわ
SOWA (FIDGET)
?

DON'T WORRY, I CAN CARRY THEM.
FURU (SHAKE)
ふる
HUH...? Y-YOU INSIST?
SHE'S THE QUIET TYPE...

HNNGH...
...

TOO HEAVY, RIGHT?

REALLY, I GOT THIS.

SHE WANTS TO HELP THAT BADLY?
?
BA (REACH)
ばっ

HOW ABOUT WE EACH TAKE HALF?
......

AND SINCE HER FACE CAN'T SHOW EXPRES-SIONS...

ZUUUN (GLOOM)
ず――ん...
HUH!? WHY SO GLUM!?
...EVERY DAY IS FULL OF MYS-TERIES.

WHAT'S THE ISSUE NOW...?

♪
♬

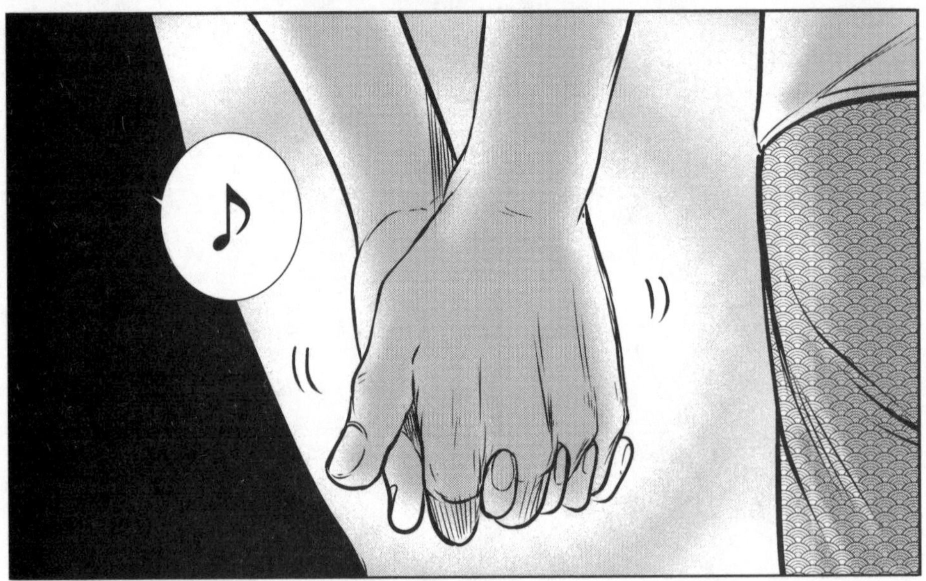
♪

♬
SHE JUST WANTED TO HOLD HANDS?
WE DIDN'T GET MUCH HAND-HOLDING IN TODAY, SINCE IT WAS SO HOT.
MM-HMM...

WHOA!?

YES, PLENTY OF MYSTERIES, BUT...

ぎゅっ GYU (SQUEEZE)

けら KERA (CACKLE)
けら KERA
T-TOO HOT FOR THAT!

ぎゅ GYUUU
CAREFUL! I'M FALLING!

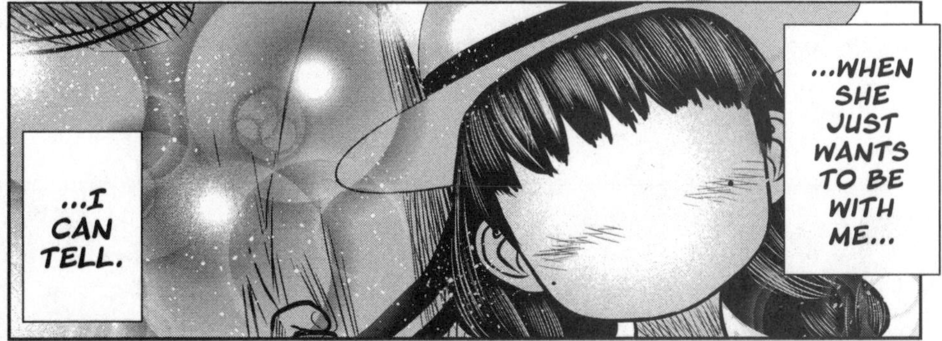
...WHEN SHE JUST WANTS TO BE WITH ME...
...I CAN TELL.

Never Want to Let You Go

♡
UM, WE'RE AT HOME NOW.
HAVING BOTH HANDS AVAILABLE WOULD MAKE THIS QUICKER, NO?

YOU'RE HAPPY, RIGHT?
HARD TO TELL...

PART 2

Her and Recharging

KOTO (KLUNK)
コト…
THE THING IS...

MORNING.
ほわ…
HOWA (DAZED)
NOT TO BRAG, BUT I'VE GOT A GIRL-FRIEND.

THANKS, AS ALWAYS! TIME TO DIG IN.
...SHE'S GOT NO FACE.

ばたん…
BATAN (SLAM)
I SHALL RETURN!
ビシッ
BISHI (SHWP)
WHEN I THINK ABOUT THEM...
...I TEND TO WONDER HOW...
...THEY DON'T RUN OUT OF ENERGY.
BESIDES JUST MY GIRL-FRIEND...
...THIS TOWN IS FULL OF OTHERS...
...WHO DON'T EVER NEED TO EAT.
DELISH!

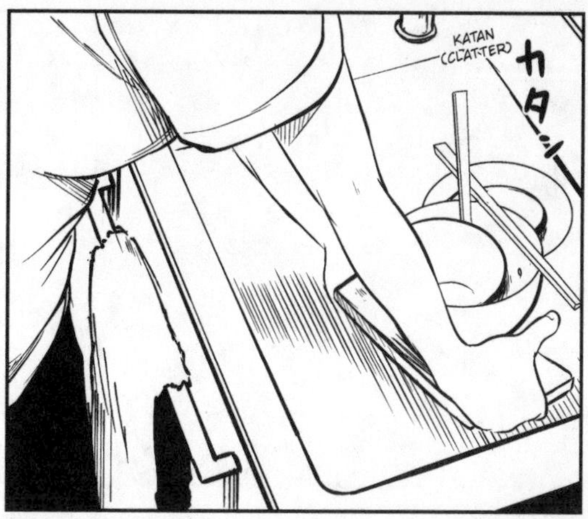
KATAN (CLATTER)
カタン

GOSHI
ごし
GOSHI (SCRUB)
ごし

PA (SHWP)
パッ
PA
パッ
ふき
FUKI (WIPE)
ふき
FUKI
TA (TMP)
タタタ
TA
TA

GADAN
ガダン
GADAN (RATTLE)
ガダン
GODO
ゴド
GODO
ゴド
ゴド
GODO (RUMBLE)
ガダッ
GADAN

PA (FWAP)
ぱっ
PA
ぱっ

PINPOOON (DING-DONG)
ピンポーン
......

YOU'VE, UH, WON SOME SORT OF CONTEST YOU ENTERED ......
お米プレゼント 選ばれました

ARMBAND: ZABO DELIVERY / BAG: BAG O' RICE GIFT

HNNGH.
HNNGH.

TRANSFERRING OVER
ザー
ZAAA (FSSHH)

カー
KAAA (CAW)
ヤー
KAAA
ヤー
KAAA

......
......
とぼ
TOBO (TODDLE)
とぼ
TOBO

I'M HOME!
ENERGY METER
MAX
KYUUU (DRAIN)

HOLY COW!!
GYU (GLOM)
ぎゅ
BWUH!?

C'MERE, YOU.
ぎゅんっ
KYUN (ZOOP)
SHE MAY NOT HAVE A FACE, BUT...

SURI (RUB) すり
SURI すり
SURI すり
MY TURN TO GETCHA BACK! TAKE THIS!
!

... WEIRDLY ENOUGH, AROUND ME...
PAAAA (BEAM)
ぱあぁぁ

...IT SEEMS LIKE...
OH! WE'RE DANCING NOW?
♪
...SHE'S ALWAYS SMILING.

Smiles
WHEN WE'RE TOGETH-ER...
...THAT'S THE MOST NOURISHING THING FOR HER.

Her and a Nap

NOT TO BRAG, BUT...
...I'VE GOT A GIRL-FRIEND.

THE THING IS...
...SHE'S GOT NO FACE.

SIGNS: REAL ESTATE, LOTS OF LOTS FOR YOU / ZABO TOWN

HER LACK OF A FACE...
...GIVES RISE TO LOTS OF MYSTER-IES.
IS SHE ASLEEP? CAN'T TELL......
ODEN

かくんっ
KAKUN (SLUMP)
......

はっ
HA (GASP)
!

OH?
かっくんっ
KAKKUN

NEVER SEEN THAT BEFORE...

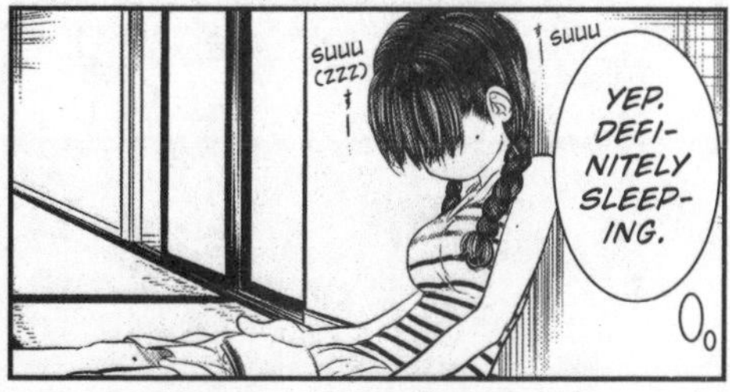
SUUU
SUUU (ZZZ)
YEP. DEFI-NITELY SLEEP-ING.

BETTER BRING HER A BLANKET...

......
SOOOO (DRAPE)
そ——...

SOUND ASLEEP...

WHY DON'T I SLEEP OUT HERE TONIGHT TOO...?

OH!
POSU (FWMP)
ポスッ

SUUU
SUUU

......I DON'T USUALLY MAKE A POINT OF STARING, BUT...

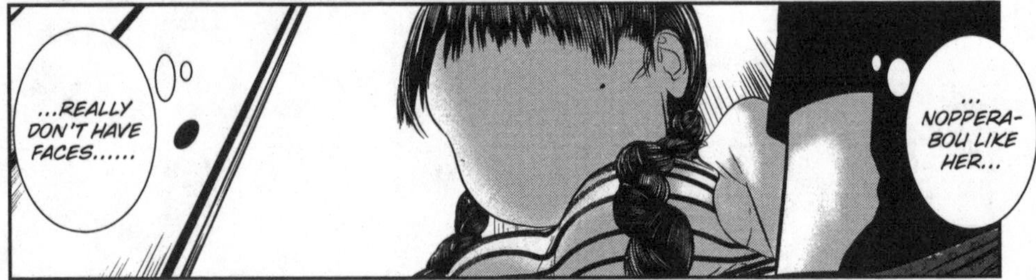
... NOPPERA-BOU LIKE HER...
...REALLY DON'T HAVE FACES......

LOVELY SKIN, THOUGH.

どき
DOKI
......
どき
DOKI (BADUM)

I LOVE YOU.

MAKES ME BLUSH EVEN IN HER SLEEP.
HA-HA-HA...
I COULD NEVER TELL HER WHILE SHE'S AWAKE.

KAAAAA (BLUUUUSH)
かあぁぁぁ....

WHOA!? YOU'RE AWAKE!?
WOWWWWW.
BA (BWAM)
EVERY DAY WITH HER...
...IS FULL OF MYSTERIES, BUT...
HUH!? YOU WANNA HEAR IT AGAIN? TH-THAT'S EMBARRASSING.
..."HAPPINESS" IS CLEAR ENOUGH.

SLEEPING FOR REAL NOW...?
CAN'T TELL...

Her and a Fight......!?

カン
KAN (KLANG)
カン
KAN
カン
KAN
NOT TO BRAG, BUT I'VE GOT A GIRL-FRIEND.
ガチ
GACHI (KACHK)

WELCOME BACK!
YOU SURE ARE GETTING HOME LATE, YOUNG MAN!
MY WORK IN THE HUMAN REALM RAN LONG...
GET HOME SAFE, OKAY? ♪

!
THE THING ABOUT HER IS...

...SHE'S GOT NO FACE.

...

GO (DOOM) ゴ GO ゴ GO ゴ GO ゴ GO ゴ GO ゴ...

PLUS, SINCE SHE'S SO QUIET BY NATURE...

...I DEAL WITH PLENTY OF MYS-TERIES.

FOR INSTANCE, TODAY... SHE'S IN A FOUL MOOD? ...I THINK...?
?

バッ BA (FWIP)
I-I'M BACK.
!

!?
!?
SA (SHWP) さっ
SA さっ

Y-YOU WON'T LET ME IN?
KOKURI (NOD) こくり

BA (FWP)
!?

TON (TAP) とん
TON とん
!?

SHOOT ...
WAS TODAY SOME KINDA ANNIVERSARY?
FOR THE LIFE OF ME, I CAN'T REMEMBER...!

THE DAY WE STARTED DATING ...? NO, THAT'S NOT IT ...
WAIT. DID I MAKE SOME SORTA BIG PROMISE TO HER...?
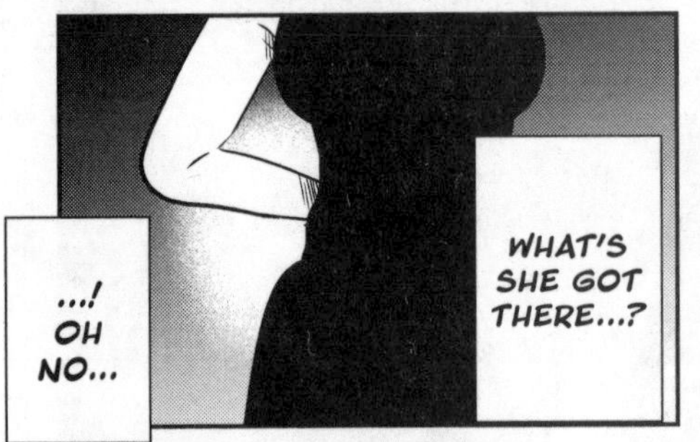
WHAT'S SHE GOT THERE...?
...! OH NO...

IS THIS A PROBLEM...?
...SHE DID GET MAD ABOUT MY FIGURE COLLECTION ...
MAYBE SHE FOUND OUT I'M STILL COLLECTING ON THE DOWN-LOW ...!?

CHI (TICK)
CHI
CHI
PI (BEEP)
PI
PI
PI
PI
SA (RSTL)
SA

PAN (POP)
パ
ン
ッ

......?

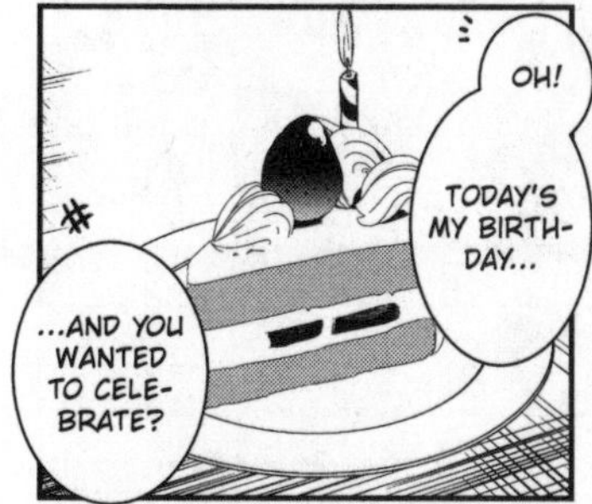
OH!
TODAY'S MY BIRTH-DAY...
...AND YOU WANTED TO CELE-BRATE?

NADE
なで
NADE (PAT)
なで

NADE
なで
NADE
なで
I'VE BEEN SO BUSY LATELY, IT SLIPPED MY MIND.
WELL, GEEZ ...
THANKS.
なで
NADE

WERE YOU WORRIED ?
MM-HMM...
TODAY WAS ANOTHER-ER DAY...

...FULL OF MYS-TERIES WITH HER.
THANK YOU.
BUT THE FACT THAT SHE CARES ABOUT ME IS SOME-THING...
...I KNOW FOR SURE.

She Sees All

THIS IS THE ONE I COULDN'T GET MY HANDS ON!
IS IT REALLY OKAY!?
SHE KNEW I DIDN'T QUIT COLLECTING.
I'VE GOT PERMISSION NOW.

Her and the T-Shirt

JIME (DAMP)
じめ…
UGH... THESE ARE NEVER GONNA DRY...
AND HERE I AM, WITHOUT CLEAN CLOTHES FOR TOMORROW ...

NOT TO BRAG, BUT I'VE GOT A GIRL-FRIEND.
ZAAAAA (FSSHH)
THE THING IS, SHE'S GOT...

...NO FACE.
BA (FWAP)
バッ
OH!? WHAT'S THAT!? YOUR WALLET!?

YOU WANNA BUY ME SOME NEW DUDS!? SWEET!
♪

SINCE SHE HAS NO FACIAL EX-PRESSIONS TO READ...
YAY, RAIN!!

座坊洋品店
...AND SINCE SHE'S PRETTY QUIET ALREADY, I'M OFTEN LOST...
FURU ふる
FURU (SHAKE) ふる
EH? NO GOOD...?
×
SIGN: WESTERN-STYLE CLOTHING SHOP

HOW ABOUT THIS? NICE AND SIMPLE.

THIS, THEN!
FURU ふる
FURU ふる
SALE

O-OKAY, HOW ABOUT SOMETHING DIFFERENT FROM MY USUAL!?
FURU ふる
FURU ふる
SALE
ZABO THE ROCK

WH-WHAT ABOUT THIS ONE!?
BURU ブル
BURU (SWIVEL) ブル
BURU ブル
BURU ブル
...WHEN WE TRY TO COMMUNI-CATE.

YOU FINDING EVERYTHING ALL RIGHT ......?
NO STAMP OF APPROVAL YET...
!

!
CHON (POKE)
ちょん
ちょん
CHON

HMM?
THIS ONE?
KOKURI (NOD)
コクリ。
THIS IS THE ONE FOR ME?

BUN (SWING)
ブン
WHY NOT THIS? IT'S GOT A SIMILAR DESIGN.
AND I LIKE CATS...
BUN
NAKO

......? WHY'S SHE INSISTING ON THAT ONE?
GUI (SHUV)
GUI

SURE, THEN. IF IT'LL MAKE YOU HAPPY.
YAA AY!!
YOU GOT IT, SIR.

THE NEXT DAY
MIIIN (BZZZZ)
MIN
MIIIN

I GET IT.

YOU ALREADY HAD THE SAME SHIRT.

♪

SPEAKING OF, I GUESS WE NEVER HAD MATCHING OUTFITS.

PON (PRESS)
ぽんっ
♡
SHE CAN'T TALK OR MAKE FACES, BUT STILL...

WE MAKE QUITE THE PAIR. ❤
...WE GET EACH OTHER.

Quite the Pair

WE'RE PRETTY DIFFERENT, AND YET...
I KNOW YOU'RE NOT ORIGINALLY FROM THESE PARTS, SIR, BUT...
...YOU TWO HAVE GOT THE SAME VIBE GOING ON.
LIKE A COUPLE THAT'S MEANT TO BE TOGETHER. ♪
R-REALLY? YOU THINK SO!?

Her and the Petting

NOT TO BRAG, BUT...
GOOD EVENING.
MEOW...
MEOW...
...I'VE GOT A GIRL-FRIEND.

MEOW...
MEOW...

NADE
NADE (PET)
THE THING ...
... ABOUT HER IS...

MEOW...
MEOW...
MEOW...
MEOW...

... SHE'S GOT NO FACE.

BATAN (SHUT)
バタッ
I'M HOOOME! ♪
HER QUIET NATURE AND LACK OF A FACE MEAN THAT EVERY DAY WITH HER...

...THE CUTEST?
AREN'T YOU...
NADE
NADE
NADE
NADE
NADE
NADE
NADE
なでなでなで
MUST BE NICE...

...IS FULL OF MYSTERIES ... ... ABOUT HER NEEDS AND WANTS.
SU (SWF)
NADE なで
なで NADE (PET)

...?
...
ARE YOU... BOWING ...?

PEKO (BOW) ペコ
HOW FORMAL OF HER.
VERILY, I HATH ARRIVEST HOME.

?
BUN (SHAKE) ブン
BUN ブン
THAT'S NOT IT?

-SNIFF-
-SNIFF-
NADE なで
なで NADE

BA (FWOOP) ばっ
!!
YOU SMELL NICE, AS ALWAYS.

? STILL WRONG ?
...

ごろんっ
GORON (FWUMP)

ごろ
GORO (ROLL)
ごろ
GORO
......

HUH!?
じーっ
JIII (STAAARE)

WHAT THE HECK DOES SHE WANT FROM ME?
QUITE THE BRAIN-TEASER...
FURI フリ
FURI (WAG) フリ

わく WAKU
わく WAKU (EXCITED)
SLEEPING ......? IS SHE EXHAUSTED?

I'LL TAKE CARE OF THE DISHES! YOU RELAX!
AAH...!!

......? HUH? THAT'S NOT IT EITHER?
SHUN (GLOOM) しゅん...

ALL DONE IN HERE.
......
KYU (SQUEAK)
きゅ

SCRITCHIES, PLEASE!
MM!
!?
FINAL ATTEMPT

UMM ...
SORRY, NO CLUE...

HOW ABOUT THIS?

かあああああ....
KAAAAAA (BLUUUUUSH)
WELL? NAIL ON THE HEAD?

AWAWAWA (SQUEEEEE)
あわわわわわ
?
HUH? SHE'S FLUS-TERED—SO THAT STILL WASN'T IT?
WAWAWA
AS USUAL, EACH DAY WITH MY FACELESS GIRL-FRIEND...

...IS FULL OF MYS-TERIES.

Getting What She Wants Somehow

IN THE END...
NYAN (MEOW)
にゃんっ♥
I'M HOME—
WHOA!?
なでなで希望!
IN DESPERATE NEED OF PET-PETS!
...SHE GOT THE PETS SHE WANTED.

Her and Outerwear

READY TO HEAD OUT?
NOT TO BRAG, BUT I'VE GOT A GIRL-FRIEND.

TA (TMP)
TA
THE THING IS...

...SHE HAS NO FACE.

COULD BE CHILLY WHERE WE'RE HEADED. BRING A JACKET?

FURU (SHAKE)

NO.

FURU

HUH? WHY NOT ...?

JUST IN CASE? YOU DON'T WANNA CATCH COLD.

BUN (FWAP)

BUN

TH-THAT AGAINST IT?

SHE'S PRETTY QUIET, SO EVERY DAY...

FIRM NO

YOU HATE THE IDEA THAT MUCH?

...IS FULL OF MYS-TERIES.

CHAPU (PLUNK)
HMM? THIS IS WEIRD...

I'M SURE THIS IS THE RIVER KNOWN FOR FIREFLIES IN TOWN......

THEY SAY IT'S THE PERFECT LITTLE GETAWAY, SO I WAS HOPING TO SEE THOSE FIREFLIES WITH YOU ......

GATA (SHIVER)
GATA
GATA
GATA
......

IT'S CHILLY HERE EVEN IN SUMMER-TIME...
GYU (SQUEEZE)
I GUESS...... WE GOTTA RESORT TO THIS...

I TOLD YA THAT YOU SHOULD'VE WORN SOMETHING.
♪
♬

WAIT...... WHY'RE YOU ACTING SO PLEASED...?
♬
♪

GYUUU
C'MON, THIS IS A LITTLE MUCH! WE'RE OUT IN PUBLIC!
YOU'RE ALL WARMED UP NOW, RIGHT?

HEY! I CAN'T ROW WITH YOU ALL OVER ME!

ACK!? GIVE IT A REST! WE'RE GONNA GET STUCK IN THOSE BUSHES!!
GASA (RUSTLE)
GASA

THIS IS... DANGER-OUS...
!
PAAAA (GLOOOW)

ぱぁぁぁぁぁ…

PAAAAAA (GLOOOOOW)

WHOA ...!

PRETTY ...!

SINCE MY GIRL-FRIEND HAS NO FACE...
... EVERY DAY IS FULL OF MYS-TERIES, BUT...

CHON (POKE)
CHON
...SOME-HOW, WHEN WE'RE TOGETH-ER...

EH-HEH!
SURE, I GET IT NOW.

WE CAN BE LOVEY-DOVEY IN PUBLIC. SOME-TIMES.
... GOOD LUCK SEEMS TO FOL-LOW.

YOU LEAVE ME NO CHOICE...
READY TO HEAD OUT?
HMM...
GETTING THAT EMBRACE IN PUBLIC TAKES SOME ADVANCED PREP......

BUT I KNOW FOR A FACT SHE LOVES ME.

PART 3

Her and Sleeping In

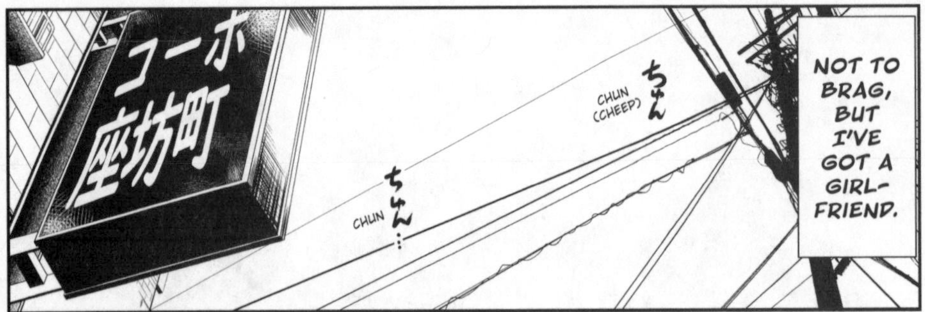
NOT TO BRAG, BUT I'VE GOT A GIRL-FRIEND.
ちゅん
CHUN (CHEEP)
ちゅん…
CHUN
コーポ座坊町

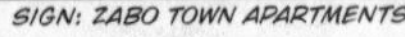
SIGN: ZABO TOWN APARTMENTS

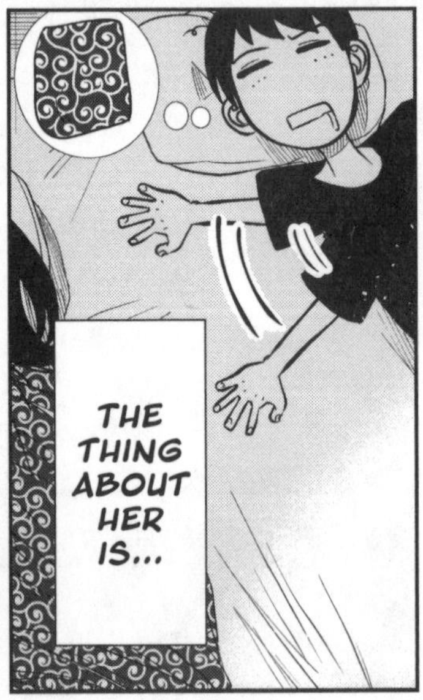
THE THING ABOUT HER IS...

... SHE'S GOT NO FACE.

IS SHE SLEEPING...? I'M SURE OF IT TODAY...
THIS HAPPENED BEFORE...

RIGHT. CHECKING HER FACE... WON'T TELL ME ...
SUUU (FWHH)
SUUU

BATH-ROOM TIME ...
EVERY DAY WITH MY FACE-LESS GIRL-FRIEND...
...IS FULL OF MYS-TERIES.

?
?

シャー
JAAA (FSSHH)

GUCHA (GARGLE)
GUCHA

シャーッ
SHAAAA (SSSHHH)

MORNIN'!
GOOD MORNING.
MORNING.

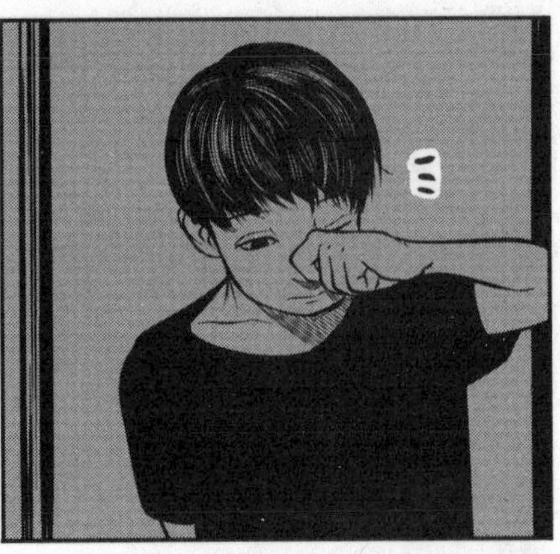

HMM ...?

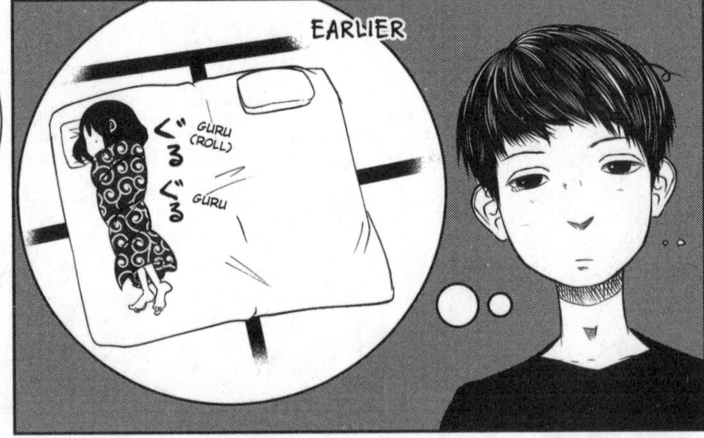
EARLIER
GURU (ROLL)
ぐるぐる
GURU

DID I WAKE YOU?
...

NAW, YOU CAN'T FOOL ME.
WITH THOSE FAKE SNORES.
GUUU (ZZZ)
ぐー
GUUU

GUUU
ぐー
GUUU
...

HUH...? SHE'S REALLY SLEEP-ING?
GUUU
GUUU

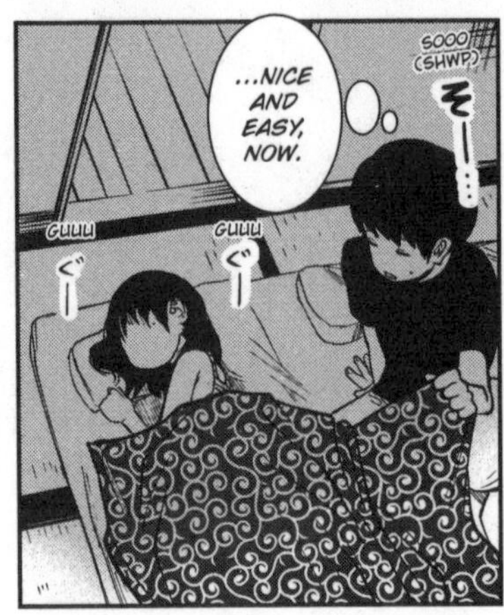
...NICE AND EASY, NOW.
SOOO (SHWP)
GUUU
ぐー
GUUU
ぐー

!
KORO
ころ
ころ
KORO (ROLL)

♪
HA. I KNEW YOU WERE AWAKE.

YES, EVERY DAY WITH HER...
WE'VE GOT NOWHERE TO BE TODAY, SO LET'S SLEEP IN......

...IS FULL OF MYSTERIES, BUT...
...HER BEING A CUTIE-PIE...
YOU SURE THIS ISN'T KILLING YOUR NECK?
KOKURI (NOD)
こくり
...IS ONE THING I KNOW FOR SURE.

Zzz Zzz

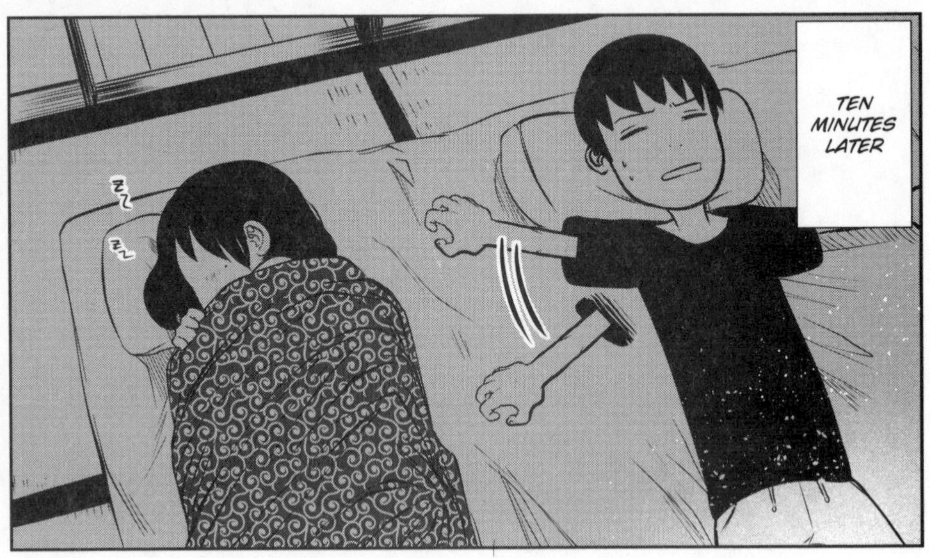
TEN MINUTES LATER

Her and the DVD

NOT TO BRAG, BUT I'VE GOT A GIRL-FRIEND.
THE THING IS, SHE'S GOT...

I'M HOME!
!
...NO FACE.

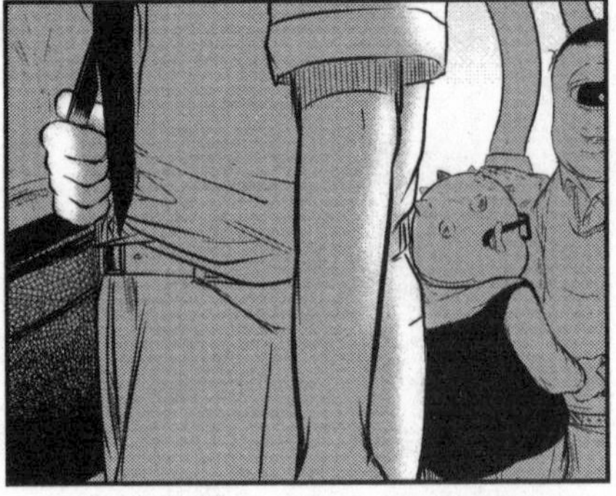

NORI (SQUIRM)
I'VE GOT SOMETHING EXCITING TODAY. ♪
NORI
NORI
NORI

ZABO RENTAL DVD
TA-DAA!
IT'S THE SEQUEL TO THAT MOVIE WE SAW! THE ONE I SAID WE SHOULD RENT NEXT!
I WAS IN THE NEIGHBOR-HOOD, SO I DECIDED TO PICK IT UP!
GEEZER MEETS MECHA-GEEZER II

TOO LAME FOR YOU?
LET'S!!
LET'S RENT THE SEQUEL ON SATURDAY?
YOU WEREN'T EXACTLY GIVING OFF STRONG VIBES DURING THE MOVIE, BUT...
...YOU CLEARLY WANTED TO SEE THE SEQUEL, RIGHT?

SINCE SHE'S GOT NO EXPRESSIONS TO READ...
SHUN (GLOOM)
しゅん...
...AND ISN'T MUCH OF A TALKER, EVERY DAY WITH HER...

!? HUH?
PEKORI (BOW)
ペコリ
SU (SWF)
すっ

SHE'S SERIOUSLY BUMMED OUT ABOUT THIS...?
...IS FULL OF MYSTERIES.

......? WELL, THAT SUCKS.

THE DISC'S REFUSING TO PLAY...
CANNOT READ DISC
NO CHOICE... I'LL HAVE TO VISIT THE RENTAL PLACE AGAIN TOMORROW...
!!

WANNA COME WITH?
I DO. ♡
SORRY... I KNOW YOU WANTED TO SEE THIS ONE.
S'OKAY!

DISC: GEEZER MEETS MECHA-GEEZER II

ちゅん...
CHUN (CHEEP)
CHUN
ちゅん...

GORGEOUS DAY, HUH? HOW ABOUT A LITTLE WALK FIRST?
POKA (SHINE)
ぽか
KOKURI (NOD)
コクリ
POKA
ぽか

GOOD MORNING, MA'AM.
MORNIN'! AREN'T YOU TWO AS CLOSE AS EVER!

HELLO THERE. ♡

WHAT A CUTIE. ♡
MEOW... ♡
MEOW... ♡

CAN I GET A SODA?

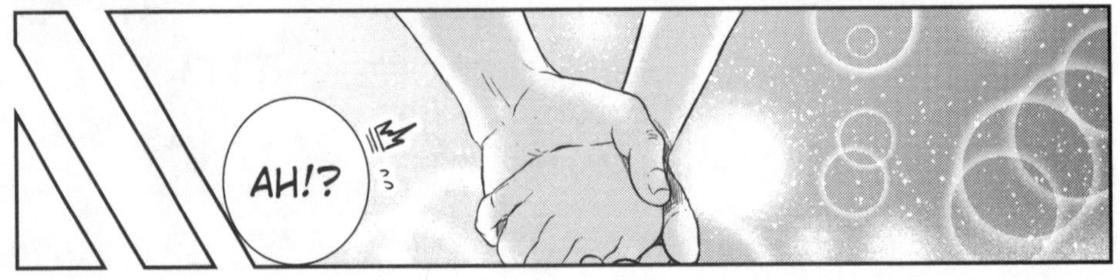
AH!?

GUH...
THE... DVD......
WE FORGOT... TO EXCHANGE IT...
AH...!!

PUSHUUU (FSSHH)
プシュー
BAN (SLAM)
バン
THE BUS ISN'T GONNA MAKE IT—
ぱたん
PATAN (SHUP)
ZABO TOWN

THE BUS IS DE-PARTING.
RIGHT ...

MY GIRL-FRIEND DOESN'T HAVE A FACE OR A VOICE, AND YET...
SQUEEZE ♥

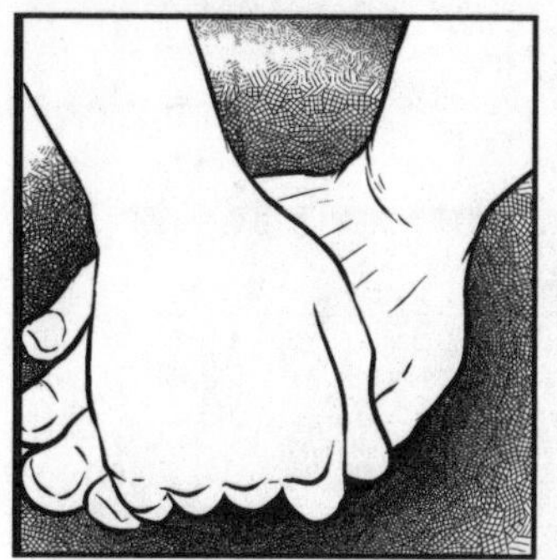

...SOME-HOW, EVERY DAY I SPEND WITH HER...

IT IS WHAT IT IS. TODAY JUST TURNED INTO A DATE DAY.
WE HADN'T HAD A DAY OUT AND ABOUT IN A WHILE, RIGHT?
BUOOOO (VROOOOM)
ブオオオ…
座坊バス
ZABO TOWN BUS
...FEELS OH SO FUL-FILLING.

Always Together

MOVIES ARE ALL WELL AND GOOD...
CLASSICS ¥50
SORRY... THIS TOOK SO MANY ATTEMPTS.
ふる FURU (SHAKE)
ふる FURU
CLASSICS ¥50
GEEZER MEETS MECHA-GEEZER II...? I THINK WE'VE GOT MORE IN STOCK...
STAFF
...BUT SPENDING TIME WITH YOU IS BEST OF ALL.

Her and a Cold......!?

YAWN...

AAH! FINALLY! A DAY OFF!

NOT TO BRAG, BUT...

カチ KACHI (CLICK)

...I'VE GOT A GIRLFRIEND.

たたっ TA (TMP) TA

ブオオオ BUOOO (VRRRM)

THIS OLD THING'S STILL KICKING.

WANNA COOL OFF WITH ME?

THE THING IS, SHE'S GOT...

...NO FACE.

くら KURA

くら KURA

PLUS, SHE'S PRETTY QUIET, SO...

?

くら KURA (WOBBLE)

くら KURA

ふっ FU (FWIP)

...EVERY DAY WITH HER IS FULL OF MYSTERIES.

ぱたーん PATAN (SPLAT)
HUH!?
......? UH...?
HEY!? YOU OKAY!? SOMEONE!! HELP!!

YOU HUMANS WOULD CALL THIS A "SUMMER COLD" AND "ANEMIA."
PHEW...
...IS THAT ALL...? IT'S NEVER HAPPENED BEFORE......
WELL, THE SYMPTOMS WOULD BE HARD TO DETECT IN THE CASE OF YOUR GAL HERE.
YEAH...SORRY FOR ALL THE SCREAMING AND PANICKING.
SOMEBODY HEEEELP!
DON'T SWEAT IT.

TAKE CARE, NOW. ♪
YOUR MEDI-CINE.
HUH!? BUT... UH...

SHE DOESN'T... NEED MEDICINE ...?
OR, LIKE, A SHOT OF SOME KIND?
NOPE, NOTHING LIKE THAT. YOUR PRESENCE SHOULD BE ENOUGH!

! YOU FEELING BETTER!?
MUKURI (RISE)
むくり。

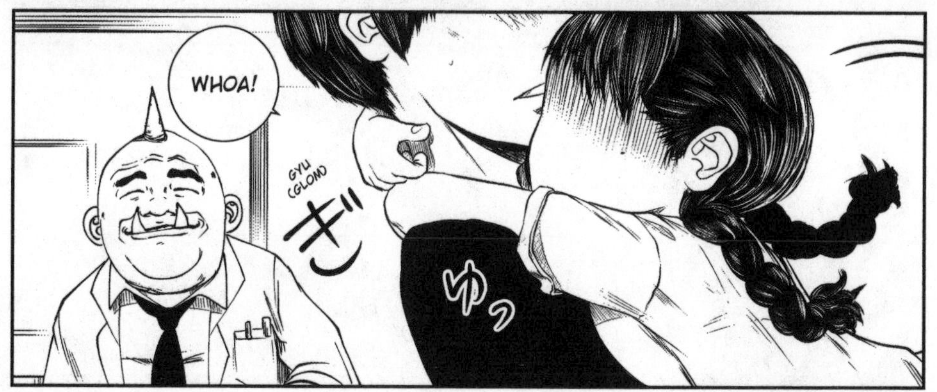
WHOA!
GYU (GLOM)
ぎゅっ

ほわっ
HOWA (GLOW)
!?

ふぁぁぁぁぁ…
FUAAAA (FWOOSH)
HUH......? WHAT IS ALL THIS...?

はあぁぁぁぁ…
PAAAAAA (SHAAAAH)
HER BODY... FEELS HOT...?

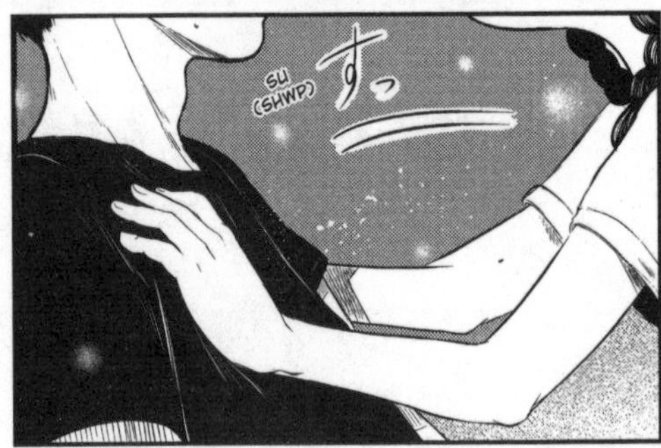
すっ
SU (SHWP)

ぐんっ
GUN (FWMP)
THERE. ALL CURED.
HUUH!? NO WAY!!

SHE SHOULD STILL GET SOME REST, THOUGH.
HANG ON! WHAT DO YOU MEAN, "CURED" !?

ISN'T IT......A COLD...?
IN HUMAN TERMS, YES.

HAVE YOU NOT BEEN SPENDING MUCH TIME TOGETHER LATELY, BY CHANCE?

WELL...... I GUESS...... IT'S BEEN A WHILE SINCE I HAD A REAL DAY OFF......

SHE DOESN'T SEEM TO BE JUST PUTTING ON A BRAVE ACT......

MY GIRLFRIEND HAS NO FACE.

SORRY FOR ALL THE TROUBLE.
PEKORI (BOW)
ペコリ
NOT AT ALL. TAKE CARE.
SO EVERY DAY WITH HER IS FULL OF MYSTERIES.
THAT WAS WILD. I DIDN'T KNOW YOU COULD DO THAT.

AND IT SEEMS I STILL HAVE PLENTY...
ZABO TOWN FIRST WARD
IT'S GREAT THAT YOU HEALED SO QUICKLY. LET'S HEAD HOME AND RELAX?
...TO LEARN ABOUT HER.

Still Plenty to Learn

FIRST, AN INCREASE IN CUDDLE TIME.
SURI (NUZZLE)
SURI
TH-THIS IS ILLNESS PREVENTION, RIGHT? RIGHT?

Her and the Inn

NOT TO BRAG, BUT...
座坊旅館
座坊旅館
...I'VE GOT A GIRL-FRIEND.
SIGN: ZABO INN

WOW! NICE, BIG ROOM.
THE THING ABOUT HER IS, SHE'S GOT...
TA TA TA TA (TMP)

♪
...NO FACE.

SHE CAN'T MAKE FACIAL EXPRES-SIONS...
...AND SHE'S ON THE QUIETER SIDE TO START WITH...
♪
BIG GARDEN TOO.

I'M GLAD WE GOT SUCH A NICE ROOM HERE. ♪
...BUT WEIRDLY, I CAN USUALLY TELL HOW SHE'S FEELING.

SLEEPY?
AH!!

!
KOTEN (BONK)
コテン

THERE'S ALWAYS TOMORROW, SO LET'S GET SOME SLEEP.

TIRED FROM THE TRIP?
RUB
RUB

GOOD NIGHT! CAN'T WAIT FOR TOMORROW.

......
......

...

GOSO
GOSO (SQUIRM)

GORO (ROLL)
...
GORO

CAN'T SLEEP...
......

......
......

WANNA C'MERE?
PA (SPREAD)
ぱっ

I ALSO HAVE A TOUGH TIME SLEEPING IN A STRANGE BED...
SO YEAH, I SAW YOU TOSSING AND TURNING ......

AAH! THIS IS MUCH COMFIER, DON'CHA THINK? JUST THE THING TO CALM US DOWN!
MY FACE-LESS GIRL-FRIEND ...

...CAN'T MAKE FACES OR SPEAK, BUT...
.....OKAY. NOW IT'S HOT...
KOKURI (NOD)
こくり

...WE TRUST EACH OTHER.
BUT LET'S STAY LIKE THIS TONIGHT, OKAY?

With You at My Side......

OUR LITTLE TRIP ENDED YESTERDAY, THOUGH! YOU STILL CAN'T SLEEP?
I FEEL CALMEST CUDDLING WITH YOU.

Her and Her Friend

MY GIRL-FRIEND HAS NO FACE.
YOU'RE IN A GOOD MOOD.
RUN (BOP) るん
RUN るん

DESPITE HER LACK OF A VOICE AND FACIAL EXPRES-SIONS...
YOU HAVEN'T SEEN ONIKO-CHAN IN A WHILE, RIGHT?
WAKU (EXCITED) わく
わく WAKU
...SHE HAS PLENTY OF FRIENDS.

BOTTLE: TEA

ピンポーン
PINPOOON (DING-DONG)
!!
YEAH, BE RIGHT THERE.
座坊書店
ZABO BOOKS

HEYYY, IT'S ME! I'M HERE. ♥
TA
TA (TMP)
WEL-COME.

SURI すり♡
SURI すり♡
すり♡ SURI (RUB)
NOPPE-CHAAAN. ❤❤ IT'S BEEN, LIKE, FOREVS. ♪
NYA HA HA. ♡
SHE AND ONIKO-CHAN HAVE BEEN FRIENDS FOR A LONG TIME.
THEY'RE THICK AS THIEVES.
...OR SO I THOUGHT?
HERE, BF-SAN. A GIFT WE CAN ALL SHARE. ❤
I KNOW NOPPE-CHAN LOVES THESE. ❤❤
AW, THANKS.
HOW KIND OF YOU.
!!
GASA (RUSTLE)
...HMM?
... WHAT THE HECK...?
YAP
YAP
GAB
ONE... TWO... THREE...
GAB
IT'S JUST THAT ...
... ONIKO-CHAN IS KIND OF A SPACE CASE. SHOCK-INGLY SO.
URK!? THE HANGER'S STILL IN THERE!?
CLOTHES HANGER
SFX: GUI (TUG)

HOKA (STEAM)
ほか
THESE... ARE THE OOBANYAKI CAKES YOU BROUGHT, BUT...
THERE'RE THREE OF THEM...
ほか
HOKA
SURE ARE! 'COS NOPPE-CHAN LOVES THESE THINGS! RIGHT?
HOKA
ほか
KOKURI (NOD)
コクリ
HUH!?
ほか HOKA

UM...... CAN YOU EVEN EAT STUFF ...?
HISO (PSST)
HISO
NO.
FURU (SHAKE)
ふる
DIDN'T THINK SO...
SO... WHAT, EXACTLY? ONIKO-CHAN JUST DOESN'T GET THAT ...?
FURU
ふる

PEKAAA (BEAM)
ぺか〜〜〜っ
WE USED TO CHOW DOWN ON THESE THINGS ALL THE TIME AS KIDS.
SO THIS MISUNDER-STANDING HAS LASTED FOR QUITE A WHILE...

B-BECAUSE YOU'RE CHILDHOOD FRIENDS ...?
I GOT THIS!

PAKU (MUNCH)
ぱく
PAKU
ぱく
PAKU
ぱく
PAKU
ぱく
PAKU
ぱく
SWEEEET.
...
ちら CHIRA
CHIRA (GLANCE)

ぱく PAKU
ぱく PAKU
ぱっくんっ PAKKUN
HMM?
CHON (POKE)
ちょん

HUH!? I GOT CRUMBS ON ME? GET 'EM OFF!
POFUN (PWOOF)
ポフン

MMM. ❤❤ SUCH SOFT HANDS, NOPPE-CHAN.
PA (FWUP)
パッ
パッ
PA
YOU GOT THE CRUMBS?

YES, ONIKO-CHAN CAN BE QUITE THE SPACE CASE.
WHOA!? YOU SCARFED DOWN THE WHOLE THING ALREADY!?
SERIOUSLY...?
PHEW...
TO THE EXTENT THAT I CAN'T EVEN KEEP UP......
LIKE I THOUGHT—YOU LOVE THIS STUFF, NOPPE-CHAN.
PAKKU (MUNCH)
ぱっく
PAKU
ぱく
ぱく
PAKU
UHH... SHE DIDN'T NOTICE...?
BUT, WELL...... SHE GETS ALONG JUST FINE WITH MY GIRL-FRIEND.

What You've Got That I Don't

NOPPE-CHAN, WHAT I LOVE ABOUT YOU IS HOW, UNLIKE ALL THOSE JERKS, YOU DON'T MAKE A NASTY FACE WHEN I'M BEING A BIG OL' DUMMY.
AND YOU NEVER SAY MEAN STUFF NEITHER.
THAT'S 'COS YOU'RE SUCH A SWEETIE. LOVE YA! ❤❤
THAT HELPS EXPLAIN WHY THEY GET ALONG SO WELL.

Noppeko and Oniko

ONCE UPON A TIME, THERE WAS A VERY, VERY LITTLE...

...ONI GIRL.

SHE WAS VERY LITTLE, BUT ALSO VERY STRONG.

AND SHE HAD NO FRIENDS.

I-I'M CRYIN' UNCLE... Y'GOT ME...

BUT SHE WANTED FRIENDS.

ZABO TOWN
SOME TOOK AN INTEREST IN THE LITTLE ONI, BUT—
NIYA (GRIN)
NIYA
FIGHT HIM, AND MAYBE WE'LL BE YOUR FRIENDS?

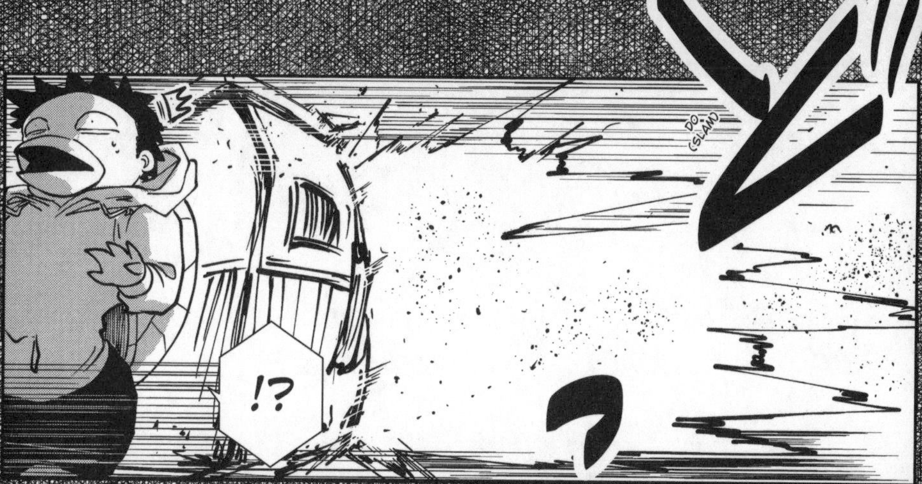
DO (SLAM)
!?

EVERY-ONE WOULD...
!
...CHANGE THE LOOK ON THEIR FACES.
W-WHUH 'APPENED?
WHOA. FOR REAL ...?
BORO
BORO (BEAT-UP)

WHEN-EVER SHE MESSED UP...

...AND THEIR EYEBALLS WOULD STARE AT HER IN RAGE.

...THEIR MOUTHS WOULD POP OPEN IN ANGER...

"YOU FOOL," "YOU IDIOT," THEY'D SAY.

THEIR MEAN WORDS HURT HER.

AND THAT'S WHY...
GU (TUG)

THAT'S DEFI-NITELY WHY...

...THESE TWO WERE ABLE TO BECOME FRIENDS.
THE OTHER GIRL HAD NO FACE.

H-HULLO.
AND NO HARSH WORDS.

BUT THERE WAS SOMETHING WARM ABOUT HER.
AND KIND.

AND SOME-HOW, THEY UNDER-STOOD EACH OTHER.

PART 4

Her and Her Job

MY GIRL-FRIEND'S WORK-PLACE IS RIGHT BELOW OUR APART-MENT.
ON MY DAYS OFF...
...I HELP OUT SOME-TIMES.
かみ ととのえます
座坊町1丁目

SIGN: WE DO HAIRDOS, ZABO TOWN FIRST WARD

SIGN: WE DO HAIRDOS

MANY IN THIS TOWN...
...ARE UNABLE TO DO THEIR OWN HAIR.

MAT: WELCOME

BANNERS: SWEET DUMPLINGS

TOILET
ちら…
CHIRA (GLANCE)
......

ぼさ…
BOSA (FRAYED)
......

HER NAME'S HANAKO.
KYU (TUG)

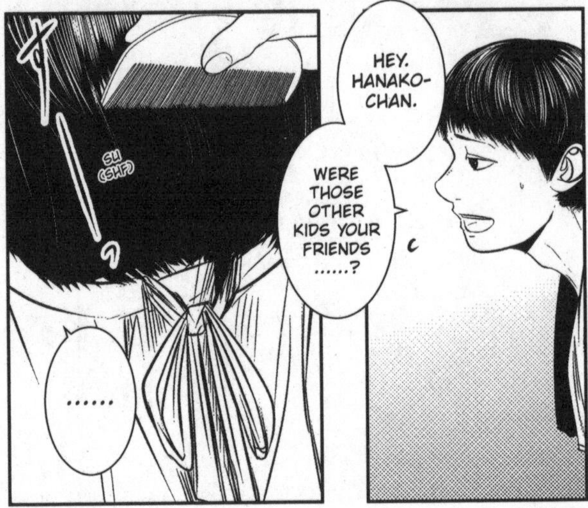
HEY. HANAKO-CHAN.
WERE THOSE OTHER KIDS YOUR FRIENDS ......?
SU (SHF)
......

HALF FRIENDS.

HANAKO-CHAN.

YOU'RE LOOKING SO PRETTY.
SARA (SHWAAH)

TA (TMP)
たっ

......
GYU (SQUEEZE)

TA
TA

!
MY GIRL-FRIEND ...
... CLEANS UP...
ぽん
PON (TAP)

...HAIR ...
...AS WELL AS THE PEOPLE AROUND HERE.
TA

SARA
SO WHERE DID YOU TWO MEET ANYWAY?

AT THE ENTRANCE TO ZABO.
WE BUMPED INTO EACH OTHER WHEN SHE WAS VISITING THE HUMAN REALM ......
SARA

♪
SARA
SARA

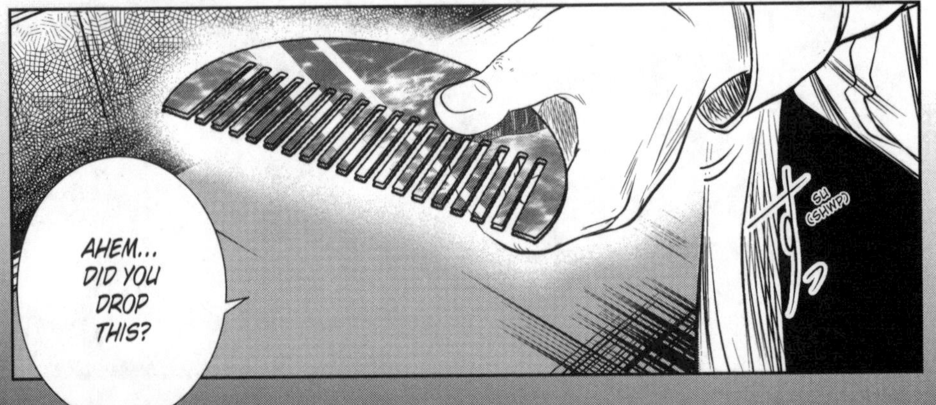
SU (SHWP)
AHEM... DID YOU DROP THIS?

I THOUGHT SHE MUST BE A MINOR CELEBRITY, WEARING A DISGUISE.

AND THEN SHE GAVE ME A BUSINESS CARD FOR THIS SHOP, AND......

SIGN: WE DO HAIRDOS, ZABO TOWN FIRST WARD

HUH!? YOU GAVE HIM A CARD LINKED TO ZABO!?
BIKU (JOLT)
...I GUESS SHE JUST WANTED TO THANK ME SOME-HOW......

SARA (SHWAAH) さら

SHE IS HOW SHE IS, BUT YOU SERIOUSLY LET YOUR GUARD DOWN TOO EASILY......

UH... YOU MIGHT BE RIGHT...

YOU WEREN'T SCARED?
HMM...
SCARED...... YOU SAY...?

♪
....
♫
SARA さら
SARA さら

SIGN: ZABO TOWN

NOT AT ALL!

YOU'LL MAKE A FINE MAN AND WIFE.
!
!?

Y-YOU REALLY THINK SO...?
WELL, OF COURSE.

AND MY PROPHECIES ARE ALWAYS ON THE MOOONEY.
KAAA
KAAA (CAW)

KUDAN

A YOUKAI WITH A HUMAN HEAD AND A COW'S BODY, WHOSE PROPHECIES ALWAYS COME TRUE. LEGEND STATES THAT THE KUDAN WILL MAKE PREDICTIONS CONCERNING VIOLENCE AND CALAMITY BEFORE DROPPING DEAD.

THAT SAID, THE KUDAN IN ZABO TOWN IS FAMOUS FOR ONLY MAKING POSITIVE, GOOD-NEWS PROPHECIES. AND SHE'S NEVER WRONG.

FUN FACT: IN ZABO TOWN, THEY REFER TO THE NOPPERA-BOU GIRL AS THE "HAIRDRESSING MASTER." MUCH LIKE THE KUDAN, MANY OF ZABO'S RESIDENTS HAVE A HARD TIME MANAGING THEIR OWN HAIR, SO SHE'S THERE TO LEND THEM A HAND.

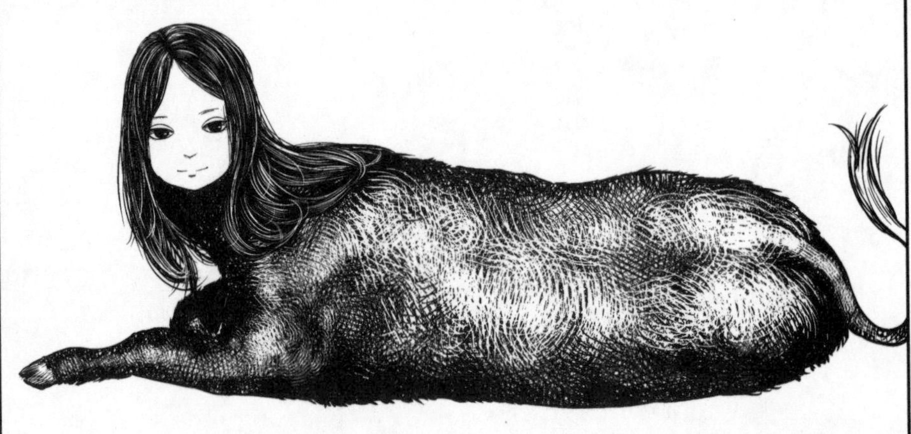

Her and Expressions

NOT TO BRAG, BUT...
...I'VE GOT A GIRL-FRIEND.
ちりん
CHIRIN
ちりん
CHIRIN (JINGLE)
OOF.

じっ…
JI (STARE)
THE THING IS...
...SHE'S GOT NO FACE.
ちりりん
CHIRIRIN
......
...
......

SHE'S NOT A BIG TALKER EITHER, SO...
WHAT'S SHE STARING AT...?
YO.
GOOD MORNING.
...LIFE WITH HER IS FULL OF MYS-TERIES.

SOME-TIMES, I FIND HER...

...JUST SITTING ......
...
...AND STARING OUTSIDE.

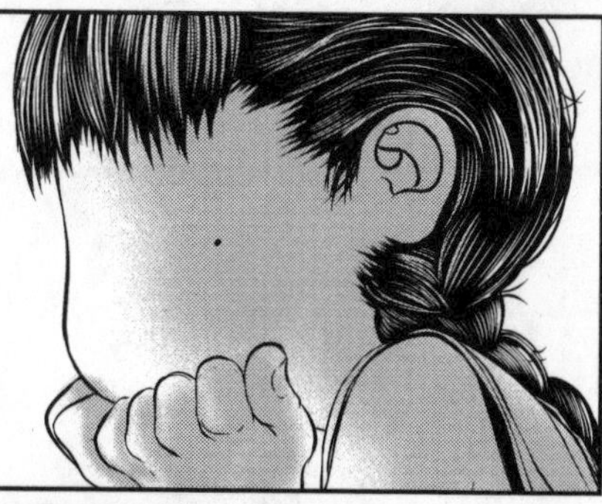
WHAT COULD A NOPPERA-BOU LIKE HER...
...BE STARING AT? I HAVEN'T THE FAINTEST.

IF ONLY SHE HAD A FACE TO READ...
......
HRM...

SOME-TIMES, I FIND MYSELF FRUS-TRATED.

SHE'S NOT MAD AT ME, RIGHT?
ちょん CHON
ちょん CHON (POKE)

WHAT?
AH. SORRY, IT'S NOTH-ING.
DIDN'T MEAN TO BOTHER ...
NOT IN A BAD MOOD, I GUESS ......?

......
CHIRIN (JINGLE)
......

SFX: MOYA (WORMP) MOYA MOYA MOYA
WHAT SORT OF FACE...
...WOULD SHE BE MAKING NOW...?

IS SHE LAUGHING ......?
TOO QUIET FOR THAT...

BROODING ABOUT SOMETHING SAD...?
NO, IT DOESN'T SEEM LIKE SHE'S...
...DOWN IN THE DUMPS...

WHAT SORT OF FACE...?
MAYBE... THIS KIND? OR THAT KIND...?
WHOOPS. YOU CAUGHT ME.
KERA (CACKLE)
けら
KERA
けら
KERA
けら
MAYBE MORE LIKE THIS...

YES, MY GIRL-FRIEND HAS NO FACE.
KERA (CACKLE) けら
KERA けら
OKAY, THAT'S DEFINITELY A LAUGH ...

BUT WHAT'S SHE LOOKING AT?
WHICH MEANS THERE ARE...

......

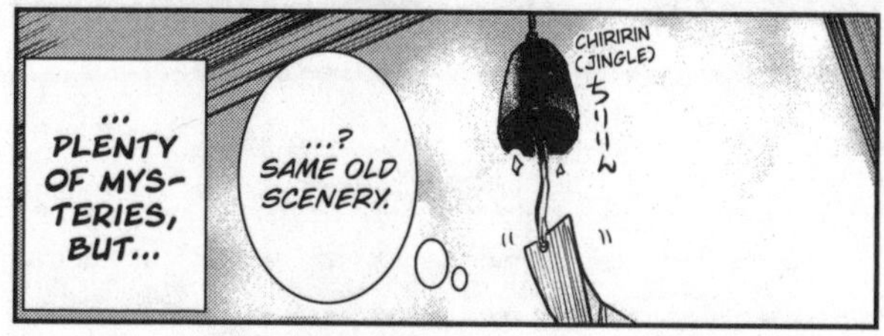
CHIRIRIN (JINGLE) ちりりん
...? SAME OLD SCENERY.
... PLENTY OF MYS-TERIES, BUT...

?
CHON (POKE) ちょん
CHON ちょん

?
?
?
BA (FWOOP) バ
...SOME-HOW, EVERY DAY WITH HER...

...! ARE YOU IMITATING THAT ONE FACE I WAS MAKING?
KOKU
KOKU
KOKU (NOD)
WAS IT REALLY THAT GOOFY?
...IS A BARREL OF LAUGHS.

She's Definitely Smiling

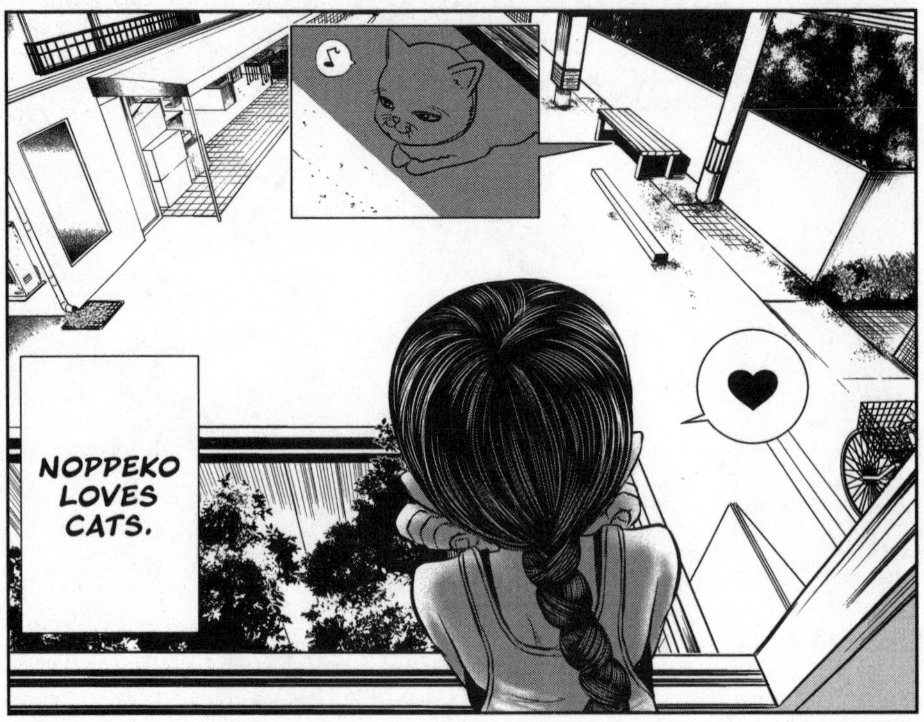
NOPPEKO LOVES CATS.

Her and the Festival

NOT TO BRAG, BUT I'VE GOT A GIRLFRIEND.
......
ZABO TOWN FESTIVAL NOTICE

ZABO TOWN FESTIVAL NOTICE
Time: 8/28, at 6:00 p.
Place: Zabo Shrine
Schedule:
6:00~ Festiva
THE THING IS, SHE'S GOT...

♪
...NO FACE.

WORK'S GONNA HAVE ME RUNNING LATE, SO LET'S JUST MEET THERE!
KOKURI (NOD)
こくり
...

BEYOND HER LACK OF FACIAL EXPRESSIONS...
PIIN (DING)
ぴーーん
...SHE'S ALSO ON THE QUIET SIDE.

TA (TMP) TA
たたっ
♪

GAYA (GAB)
がやがや
GAYA
WAI (YAP)
わいわい
WAI
座坊町祭り

SIGNS: ZABO TOWN FESTIVAL / YAKISOBA / BABY CASTELLA / BEAN SPROUT KINGDOM / SOBA OMELET / TAKOYAKI

でんっ
DEN (BAM)

SFX: KYORO (GLANCE) KYORO

キョロ
WHERE COULD SHE BE?
WHOA!? DO I KNOW YOU!?
ぎゅっ!!
GYU (GLOMP)
ぱ。
PA (FWIP)
YOU GAVE ME A SCARE.
SUCCESSFUL SURPRISE
TA-DAA!
HEH HEH HEH.

!

わく
WAKU
わく
WAKU (EXCITED)

KIRAAAN (GLINT)
キラーン
きょろ
KYORO
KYORO
きょろ
......WHERE COULD SHE BE?

SHA (ZOOM)
シャッ
WHOA!!
SHA
SHA

SIGN: ZABO TOWN FESTIVAL

SORORI (SNEAK)
そろり...
WELP, THIS SUCKS ...
WE SHOULDA PICKED A MEETING SPOT...
SORORI
そろり...

ONE, TWO...
SU (FWP)

CHIRA (GLANCE) ちらっ...
!?
MAYBE SHE'S FARTHER INSIDE ...?

OH. THERE YOU ARE.
GIKU (JOLT)
ギクッ
...! WERE YOU GONNA SNEAK UP ON ME?
NOT A CHANCE. AS IF A MASK COULD KEEP ME FROM KNOWING IT'S YOU.

IGNORE
......
SUN (SHWP)
す
......UH.
ん...

YOU... ARE MY GIRL-FRIEND, RIGHT?
IUNNO...?
OH... THAT'S ODD.

I NEVER THOUGHT I'D FIND SOMEONE ELSE AS CUTE AS HER......

!?

MY GIRL-FRIEND MAY HAVE NO FACE, BUT...
JI (STARE)
じっ...
......
......
...I KNOW HER BETTER THAN ANYONE.

GEEZ, YOU'RE EXTRA CUTE, AREN'T YOU?
ぼっ
BO (PWOOF)

I MEAN, WHEN SHE'S THAT CUTE? C'MON.
WOWWWWW.
DA (DASH)
だっ
ACK! WAIT UP!!
PYUUU (ZOOOP)
ぴゃーっ

Because I Love Everything About You

JUST WHAT IS SO CUTE ABOUT HER?
UMMM... EVERYTHING, I GUESS?

Her and Strategizing

NOT TO BRAG, BUT...... I'VE GOT A GIRL-FRIEND.
...?

UZU (FIDGET)
うず
UZU
うず
?
THE THING IS, SHE'S GOT...

...NO FACE.
UZU
うず
UZU
うず
UZU
うず
?
PLUS, GIVEN HER QUIET PERSON-ALITY...
WHAT'S WITH THE FIDGETING?
...I RUN INTO PLENTY OF MYS-TERIES IN OUR EVERYDAY LIVES.

...?
UZU
うず
UZU
うず

NOT TO BRAG, BUT...
...I'VE GOT A BOY-FRIEND.
?
?
THERE'S NO EASY WAY TO READ MY FACE OR EMOTIONS, BUT...
うず UZU (FIDGET)
...HE WORKS SO HARD TO UNDERSTAND ME, WHICH BASICALLY MAKES HIM THE BEST EVER.
UZU うず

...BUT...
ちら CHIRA (GLANCE)

NEED TO PEE?
......

...THERE ARE STILL TIMES WHEN OUR SIGNALS GET CROSSED.
MOJI (SQUIRM) もじ
?
もじ MOJI
AND THE THING IS... RIGHT NOW...

...I REALLY JUST WANNA SNUGGLE!
UZU うず
もじ MOJI
MOJI もじ
うず UZU
I-I'M LEAVING MY BACK WIDE OPEN IN THE HOPES THAT HE'LL GIMME A SQUEEZE FROM BEHIND...... THEN IT'S SNUGGLE CITY!

...BUT ME MAKING MOVES ON HIM...... WOULD BE TOO EMBAR-RASSING.
UZU うず
HRMMM.
HE'S PROBABLY JUST TIRED FROM WORK.
HOW CAN I GET WHAT I WANT...? I NEED IT TO HAPPEN... NATURALLY.
UZU うず
もじ MOJI
MOJI もじ
A SIT-UATION WHERE I'D... ... GLOM ONTO HIM...
TERRIFYING!! TOP TEN HORROR MOVIES
HA-HA-HA!
SCARY!!
GEEZ, YOU'RE CUTE.
SFX: KYUUU (HUUUG)

GRAAAAAAAAAH!!
...! THAT'S IT!
GU (CLENCH)

WHY'D WE RENT SUCH A SPOOKY MOVIE!? I CAN'T HANDLE STUFF LIKE THIS ...
EEEEEK!!!

WAAAAAAAH!!!

SOME-ONE'S GLOM-MING.
GATA
GATA (QUIVER)
AAAH...
BUT... IT'S NOT ME...

...HANG ON. I'M A NOPPERA-BOU TO START WITH...
I'M A GENUINE YOUKAI.

DOES THAT MEAN HE'S SCARED OF ME!?
WAH!
!? WHAT'S WITH THE POSE ...!?
BA (FWAH)

TOO CUTE ......!
EH...
THAT WAS S'POSED TO SCARE HIM...

I HAVE A FACELESS GIRLFRIEND.
I HAVE THE BEST BOYFRIEND.

EVERY DAY WITH HER IS FULL OF MYSTERIES......
DON'T MIND ME...
OUR DAYS ARE FULL OF LITTLE MISUNDERSTANDINGS ......

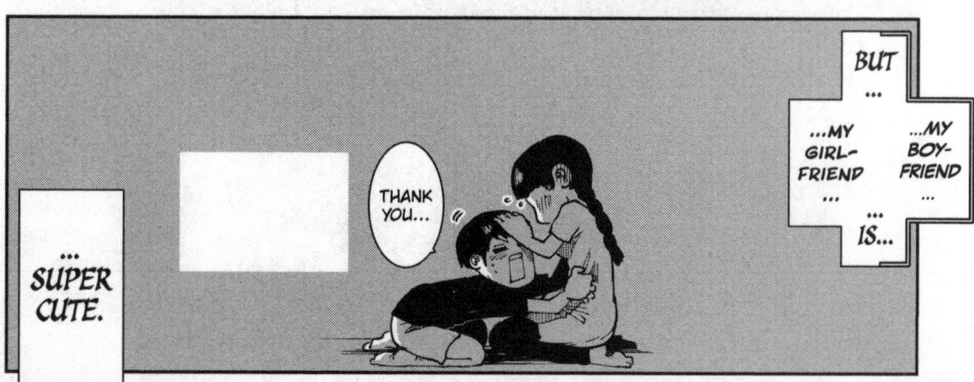
BUT ...
...MY BOYFRIEND ...
...MY GIRLFRIEND ...
IS...
THANK YOU...
... SUPER CUTE.

We Both Fidget

GUH...... TOO SPOOKY IN THERE AFTER THAT MOVIE...
UZU
うず
UZU (FIDGET)
うず
C'MON! IT'S FINE!!
もじ
MOJI (SQUIRM)
もじ
MOJI
WHY IS HE SO OKAY WITH ME...?

Her and Music

NOT TO BRAG, BUT I'VE GOT A GIRL-FRIEND.
HM-HMM.
HM-HMM.

NORI
NORI (SWAY)
THE THING IS, SHE'S GOT NO FACE.
NORI

SINCE SHE'S SO QUIET AND CAN'T MAKE FACES...
PAIN IN THE ASS...
I'VE BEEN LISTENING TO THIS ONE SONG DURING MY COMMUTE LATELY.

...IT'S OFTEN HARD FOR US TO COMMUNI-CATE.
OH! COUPLE EAR-PHONES!
WANNA LISTEN?
KOKURI (NOD)

BUT WE STILL HAVE LOTS OF FUN TOGETHER.
OH! SHALL WE DANCE?
NORI
NORI
NORI

NEVER REALIZED QUITE HOW GOOD IT WAS.
MAYBE 'COS I WAS ALWAYS LISTENING TO IT ALONE?

WOWEE! THIS SONG IS A BANGER!
DO (FWMP)
どっ

HMM...
AH! I WANNA KNOW WHAT SONGS YOU LIKE, NOPPE-CHAN!
THEN WE CAN LISTEN TOGETHER! IT'LL BE FUN!

BUT EVEN A SONG YOU WOULDN'T REALLY NOTICE IS AWESOME WHEN WE'RE LISTENING TOGETHER. ♪
THERE'S JUST SOMETHING ABOUT THAT. ♪
TEE HEE HEE.

OH! MAYBE YOU'RE NOT TOO FAMILIAR WITH HUMAN SONGS?

PIIIN (DING)
OH?

HMM? WHAT'S UP?
?

OF COURSE, THERE ARE TIMES...
BATAN (SLAM)
?? WHERE'RE WE GOING ...?

...WHEN I HAVE NO CLUE...
ZABO TOWN BUS

SFX: ZUN (TROT) ZUN

...WHAT SHE'S THINK-ING.

S-SERIOUSLY, WHAT'S GOING ON? WHY'D WE COME HERE ......?
SHHH.
GASA (RUSTLE)

?
WHAT NOW?
SU (FWP)

RIN
RIN (KREEE)
!
...?

RI (KREEE)
RI
RI
RIN
RI
RI
RI
RI
RI
RI
RI
RIN

THE CRICKETS... THEY'RE SO LOUD ...
RI
RI
RI
RIN
RIN
RIN
BUT EVEN IF I'M CLUE-LESS AT TIMES...
KOKU (NOD)
KOKU

RI
RI
RI
RIN
THIS IS DEFINITELY A SONG I WOULDN'T NOTICE NORMALLY ...
...BUT IT'S GREAT TO LISTEN WITH YOU. ♪
...OUR DAYS TOGETHER ARE ALWAYS LOTS OF FUN...
RI
RI
RIN

YOU'RE SO MATURE, NOPPE-CHAN. ♪
MY GIRL-FRIEND MAY HAVE NO FACE OR VOICE, BUT...
...AS FAR AS I'M CONCERNED, I HOPE WE'RE...
... TOGETHER FOREVER.

Let Me Hear Your Timbre

PLEASE LISTEN TO THAT WHEN YOU'RE ALONE......
I love you. I love you. I love you. I love you...
HIS VOICE, RECORDED
WHOOOOOOH...

Her and the Fortune

NOT TO BRAG, BUT...
HOT DAY, HUH?
...I'VE GOT A GIRL-FRIEND.
MIN
MIIIN
MIIIN (KREEE)

THE THING IS...
...SHE'S GOT NO FACE.

PATA
TOO HOT...
PATA (FLAP)
BUUUN (VRRRM)
MELTING OVER HERE...
WHAT'S MORE, SHE'S ON THE QUIET SIDE.

OH!

SIGN: ZABO SHRINE
DIDN'T KNOW THERE WAS A SHRINE HERE.

WANNA PICK SOME LOVE FORTUNES?
恋みくじ
LOVE FORTUNE
円
YEN
♪
KOKURI (NOD)
コクリ

AH!
MAJOR LUCK!
SHE DOESN'T HAVE FACIAL EX-PRESSIONS TO READ, AND YET...

!
S-I-I-GH...
...WHEN WE'RE TO-GETHER, I CAN JUST TELL SOME-HOW.
PURU (TREMBLE)
プル
PURU
プル

MINOR LUCK
YIKES! MINOR LUCK?
GLOOM...

す――ん...
ZUUUN (WOMMMP)
DON'T WORRY! IT'S JUST A DUMB OLD FORTUNE!
AND SHE GETS DOWN IN THE DUMPS MORE THAN YOU'D THINK.

NO NEED TO BE UPSET ABOUT IT...
GAKKUSHI (SLUMP)
がっくし..

HEEE-EEEEY! NOPPE-CHAAA-AAAAN!
URGH...
!

HANG ON... ONIKO-CHAN...
WHAT A COINKY-DINK!

NOPPE-CHAN. ♪ NOPPE-CHAN. ♪ SMOOCH ♥♥♥
...
AS PEPPY AS EVER, ONIKO-CHAN ...
...

! IS HE HER BOY-FRIEND ...?
HELLO THERE.
...HEY.

THE HECK? YOU MOPING ABOUT SOMETHING, NOPPE-CHAN?
KOKURI

HMM? MINOR LUCK?
YEE-UP.

NOT QUITE THE FORTUNE YOU WERE HOPING FOR... WANNA DRAW AGAIN?
OR YOU COULD JUST TRADE WITH ME ......?
MAJOR LUCK
WHOA! YOU GOT MAJOR LUCK, BOYFRIEND-SAN? THEN EVERYTHING'S A-OKAY!
......

'COS THAT MEANS AS LONG AS YOU'RE TOGETHER, YOU'LL HAVE MAJOR LUCK AND THEN SOME!

ONI-CHAN'S LOGIC—

MAJOR LUCK < MAJOR LUCK + MINOR LUCK

AND SINCE YOU'RE OBVS TOGETHER FOREVS, THAT MEANS LOTSA HAPPINESS!

......

Y-YEAH. I GUESS...IT WORKS THAT WAY?

MY GIRL-FRIEND MAY HAVE NO FACE...

KERA (CACKLE)

KERA

SURE. WHY NOT? ♪

...BUT SHE'S BLESSED WITH A WEALTH OF EXPRES-SIONS.
IN THAT CASE, WE'D BETTER STICK TOGETHER, HUH?
KOKURI (NOD)
...AND ALL THE DAYS I'M WITH HER ARE...
...CURIOUSLY BLESSED AS WELL.
UGHHH. WHERE'S MY...
...PRINCE CHARMING, HUH? HUH?
THAT'S HOW IT FEELS TO ME.

Two Peas in a Pod

MAJOR LUCK
すり SURI (RUB)
WE'RE GONNA BE TOGETHER FOREVS TOO, RIGHT, NOPPE-CHAN? ❤❤❤
すり SURI
DON'T SWEAT IT.
... YEAH.
MINOR LUCK
IF ONLY SHE'D JUST REALIZE.

Her and Her Gaze

I'M OFF TO DO THE SHOPPING. ♪
NOT TO BRAG, BUT I'VE GOT A GIRL-FRIEND.
OH! WANNA COME WITH?
HYOKKORI (PEEK)
ひょっこり
KOKURI (NOD)
こくり
THE THING IS, SHE'S GOT...
I'LL WAIT FOR YOU TO GET DRESSED, THEN.
...NO FACE.
PLUS, SHE'S KIND OF QUIET.
GOCHIIN (BONK)
SINCE SHE'S GOT NO FACE OR VOICE, LIFE WITH HER...
BIIIIIN (RATTLE)
SIGN: ZABO TOWN SECOND WARD
PUSHAA (FSHH)
TH-THAT WAS QUITE A BONK...
SHE'S OKAY... THIS HAPPENS ALL THE TIME...
WHAT DID SHE EVEN RUN INTO...? J-JUST BE MORE CAREFUL, OKAY...?
JUT-TING OUT
座坊町二丁目
YEAH... NOT SURE HOW THAT HAPPENED ......
YOU GOOD?
KOKURI
...IS FULL OF MYS-TERIES.

MY NOPPERA-BOU GIRLFRIEND HAS NO FACE, BUT SHE DOES HAVE VISION.
SHE SHOULD HAVE, BUT......

... WHENEVER WE'RE OUT AND ABOUT TOGETHER ...
BASHAA (SPLASH)
...CRAZY THINGS SEEM TO OCCUR.
GAN (SLAM)
とびだし ちゅうい!
CHILDREN AT PLAY

SEEMS LIKE YOU'RE NOT WATCHING YOUR STEP.
BUN (SHAKE)
BUN
REALLY? YOU ARE...?

IF YOU'RE NOT FEELING WELL, WE COULD HEAD HOME?
NO! FIRM REFUSAL

O-OKAY... IF YOU'RE SURE...
WHAT NOW...? SHE CLAIMS SHE'S WATCHING WHERE SHE'S GOING, BUT......
...SHE KEEPS BUMPING INTO STUFF TODAY. LIKE, MORE THAN EVER......

IT'D BE TRICKY TO TELL EVEN IF SHE REALLY WAS FEELING SICK......
ちら
CHIRA (GLANCE)
LET'S HOPE IT'S NOTHING ...
!

JIIII (STAAAARE)

...

NOW I SEE WHERE SHE'S LOOKING !!

OH...MAYBE WHEN WE'RE OUT ON A WALK, HER GAZE IS GLUED TO ME?
BUT SHE'S NOT EVEN AWARE OF IT...? THAT'S KINDA CUTE, BUT C'MON...

Y-YOU'RE BLUSHING, Y'KNOW...
AND YOU WERE STARING AT ME...
KI (JOLT)
...!

PERA (BLAB)
PERA
IS THAT MAYBE WHY YOU KEEP BUMPING INTO STUFF......?
I MEAN, I'M FLATTERED, BUT IT'S DANGEROUS NOT TO WATCH WHERE YOU'RE GOING...
PERA
IF YOU DIDN'T EVEN REALIZE WHAT WAS HAPPENING... I GUESS YOU HAVE TO WORK ON THAT HABIT......
PERA
KAAAAA (BLUUUSH)
......

WHOA !?
DA (DASH)

G...
TA (TMP)
TA
GOOD!
FACE FORWARD AS YOU WALK!
......
HOW'S IT FEEL TO BE THE ONE GETTING STARED AT?
WELL!? MAKING YOU BLUSH EVEN MORE, RIGHT?

MY GIRL-FRIEND HAS NO FACE.
RED, RIGHT DOWN TO YOUR EARS—
GATSUN (BONK)
SHE'S GOT NO FACE OR VOICE, BUT...
AWA (FRET) WA WA
あわわわ...
PUSHUUU (SIZZLE)
...I'M REMINDED JUST HOW MUCH SHE LOVES ME...
LET'S SAVE THE STARING AT EACH OTHER FOR WHEN WE GET HOME?
KOKURI (NOD)
こくり
...EACH AND EVERY DAY.

How About This?

BECAUSE I WANT TO STARE AT YOU FOREVER.
NO THANKS.
GETTING A RIDE LIKE THIS MAKES US MOBILE ...?

Me and My Boyfriend

MORNING.
ぽけ~~
POKEEE (DAAAZE)
NOT TO BRAG, BUT I'VE GOT A BOYFRIEND.

WHER-EVER WE GO...
KOKU (NOD)
...HE'S ALWAYS THINKING OF ME.

HE'S CHEER-FUL...
...A LITTLE OBLI-VIOUS...

QUITE THE BRAIN-TEASER ...
...AND JUST SO GREAT.

THE THING IS, I'VE GOT...
...NO FACE.

?
WHATCHA LOOKING AT?
HE CAN'T TELL WHERE I'M STARING OR WHAT FACES I WOULD BE MAKING.

AND BECAUSE I'M NOT SO GREAT AT TALKING...
AH!? DON'T TELL ME!!
IS IT A COCK-ROACH!?
DID ONE FINALLY CRAWL OUT!?
AWA (FRET) WA
あわわ…

...WE OFTEN HAVE MISUNDER-STANDINGS.
SHUN (GLOOM)
しゅん…
WH-WHERE!? WHERE'S THE FOUL BEAST!?

WELP, DIDN'T SPOT A SINGLE ONE, IN THE END.

AND SINCE WE CLEANED THE WHOLE PLACE WHILE SEARCH-ING...
...ALL'S WELL THAT ENDS WELL?
......
PIKA (SPARKLE)
PIKA
PIKA
PIKA

POFUN (PWOOF)
ぽふん
...WHY DOES HE EVEN WANT TO BE WITH ME...?

MOYA (WORMP)
もや
もや
MOYA
?
WHEN WE'RE TOGETHER...
...I SOMETIMES GET TO THINKING...

THIS TOWN IS FULL OF ALL TYPES.
GIRLS WHO HE COULD UNDERSTAND WAY EASIER. WHO ARE MORE FUN THAN ME.
LOTS OF GOOD POTENTIAL GIRLFRIENDS.

OH... GOOD TO KNOW ...
...WITH A GUY WHO THINKS THE WORLD OF ME...

AND YET, HERE I AM......
FEELING UNDER THE WEATHER?
ふる
FURU
ふる
FURU (SHAKE)

I MEAN, WHY IS HE EVEN...
...WITH ME AT ALL...? THAT'S WHAT I WONDER.

FU (FWOO)
...WHILE I CAN'T EVEN TELL HIM HOW I FEEL.
DOES HE EVEN ENJOY BEING WITH ME?
...IT'S LIKE THIS UNEASY ITCH IN MY HEART.

BECAUSE ...

GYUU (SQUEEZE)

...I LOVE YOU...!

...???
... HUH?

ぽんっ
BON (PWOOF)
HUUUH!? OUTTA NO-WHERE !?

HUH? HUH?
HUH!?
WHOA!? YOU'RE AWAKE!?
あたふた
ATAFUTA (PANIC)
あわわゎ
AWA (FRET)
WA
WA

S-SORRY, IT'S JUST...
...YOU SEEMED WORRIED EARLIER ...

...SO I THOUGHT I SHOULD TELL YOU HOW I FEEL......
DOKI
ドキ
DOKI
ドキ
....
ドキ
DOKI (BADUM)
DOKI
ドキ...

...IF WE WEREN'T TOGETHER...
...I WOULDN'T GET TO SPEND DAYS LIKE THIS THINKING ABOUT SOMEONE I LOVE......
WHAT'S IN THAT HEAD OF HERS?
♪

AND WHEN I DO FIGURE IT OUT ...
SHE JUST WANTED TO HOLD HANDS?
WELL, I NEVER THOUGHT ANYTHING COULD MAKE ME SO HAPPY ......

GETTING TO EXPERIENCE ALL THOSE LITTLE MOMENTS OF JOY WITH YOU......
THAT'S WHY... I LOVE... BEING WITH YOU.

EVEN DAYS LIKE TODAY, WHEN I HAD NO CLUE WHAT YOU WERE THINKING...

A-ANYWAY! JUST THOUGHT YOU SHOULD KNOW! ...SORRY.
MY BOYFRIEND IS ALWAYS THINKING OF ME.

HE'S CHEERFUL, A LITTLE OBLI-VIOUS...
LOVE TACKLE
OOF
!?
...AND JUST SO GREAT.

SO MAYBE I DO MEAN TO BRAG, SINCE...
FULL-FACE KISSSS
INTENSE PRES-SURE!!
...I'VE GOT THE BEST BOY-FRIEND.

The GIRL WITHOUT a FACE

Bonus Comic:
Her and the Gift

SIGN: ZABO TOWN FIRST WARD

座坊町一丁目

ZABO TOWN

IT'S A REMOTE LITTLE HAMLET...

...WHERE YOUKAI LIVE.

ALL MANNER OF BEINGS LIVE IN HARMONY TOGETHER.
WAI (YAP)
わい
わい
WAI
BUT AMONG ALL THE RESIDENTS OF THIS TOWN...
OUT ON A WALK, NOPPEKO-CHAN?
!
...THE GIRL WHO GETS DOTED ON THE MOST IS...

..."NOPPEKO."
THAT'S WHAT THEY CALL THE GIRL...

OR HEADING TO MEET YOUR MAN?

...WITH NO FACE.

MY, MY... SUCH A LOVEY-DOVEY COUPLE.

SINCE SHE CAN'T MAKE FACES...
...AND SINCE SHE'S ON THE QUIET SIDE...
もじ
MOJI
もじ
MOJI (FIDGET)

ZUUUN (GLOOOM)
すーーーん…
...THE OTHER TOWNSFOLK RARELY UNDERSTAND WHAT SHE'S TRYING TO COMMUNICATE.

THAT MAKES THEM WORRY...
TOBO (TODDLE)
とぼ
TOBO
とぼ
HUH!? IGNORING US...!?

...AND DOTE ON HER EVEN MORE.
H-HAVING A BAD DAY...?
MAYBE SOMETHING HAPPENED......?

かみ ととのえます
SIGN: WE DO HAIRDOS

?

NOPPEKO-CHAN... ISN'T COMING OUT...
WHAT ARE YOU LADIES DOING ......?
AH! BUS DRIVER! POP A SQUAT AND JOIN US!
NOPPEKO-CHAN SEEMS GLOOMY TODAY.
TROUBLE WITH THE BOYFRIEND, WE'RE THINKING ...
NAW... THOSE TWO? I CAN'T IMAGINE !
AH! THERE SHE IS!

THAT ALL LOOKS MIGHTY HEAVY ......
TOBO (TODDLE)
とぼ
とぼ
TOBO
SEE? YOU EVER SEEN HER LOOKING SO LOW?
HMM... I SUP-POSE...

...SHE DOES LOOK A LITTLE...
... OUT OF SORTS ......
TERRIBLY NOSY OF US— I KNOW— BUT WE'RE WORRIED ...
WE ONLY WANT WHAT'S BEST FOR THOSE TWO KIDS......

座坊衣料品

ZABO CLOTHING

MISTER, MISTER!
YEAH?

どどっ!!
DODO (BABAM)
HAVE YOU SEEN NOPPEKO-CHAN!?
!?

DON'T SCARE ME LIKE THAT!! ...HUH? NOPPEKO-CHAN?
NO, SHE HASN'T PAID MY SHOP A VISIT!!
AND YOU HAVEN'T SEEN HER?

座坊衣料
ACTUALLY, I DID. SHE WAS HAULING SOME HEAVY LUGGAGE.
KNEW IT......

OH, AND I THINK SHE'D JUST DONE SOME SHOPPING AT THE GENERAL STORE ......
ZABO GENERAL STORE

SHE'D BOUGHT A WHOLE BUNCH OF CANDLES ......

CANDLES ......?

SALE
WHAT FOR, I WONDER?
IT'S A REAL MYSTERY...... WHATEVER SHE'S UP TO ......
WHERE'S SHE GOING...?

NOPPEKO-SAN? I SAW HER ABOUT TWENTY MINUTES AGO.
!?

WHERE WAS SHE!?
GUN (BAM)

SH-SHE GOT ON A BUS...
IN FRONT OF THE SUPER-MARKET ......
ZU (ZRM)
ZU
終点
座坊町入口
HEADED FOR WHERE!?
UM... UMM......

SIGN: LAST STOP, ZABO TOWN ENTRANCE

YOU DON'T THINK ......?
NAW... IT'S TOO SOON FOR A DECISION LIKE THAT ......
BUT WHAT ABOUT THE LUG-GAGE ...?

ZABO TOWN ENTRANCE...... THE BORDER BETWEEN HERE...
...AND THE HUMAN REALM.

THE BUS IS DE-PARTING.
AND SHE LOOKED SO DEEP IN THOUGHT.

IS THAT GIRL...... ABOUT TO LEAVE ZABO ......?
BUUUUN (VROOM)
ブゥゥゥ...

L-LET'S SPLIT UP TO SEARCH!! WE'LL CHASE DOWN THAT BUS!!
NO TIME TO LOSE!!
YOU BUNCH CANVASS BYSTANDERS!! IT'S TOO DANGEROUS FOR NOPPEKO-CHAN TO ENTER THE HUMAN REALM ALL ALONE!!
ROGER THAT...

FINALLY, WE FOUND HER ......
SHE CAME A LONG WAY...
AWA (FRET)
AWA
AWA

WE HAVE TO STOP HER FROM LEAVING!
STOP HER? BUT......
...SHE'S JUST SITTING THERE?
MAYBE SHE'S NOT ABOUT TO LEAVE ZABO AFTER ALL...?
COME ON, FOLKS. DON'T YOU THINK WE'VE...

ZORO (CROWD)
ODEN
...GONE A LITTLE OVERBOARD HERE......?

DEEP IN THE MOUNTAINS...... WITH CANDLES...... LUGGAGE...... AND A GLOOMY ATTITUDE ......?
BUT WHAT COULD SHE BE DOING OUT HERE?

...SOMETHING UNSETTLING, MAYBE...?
GO (DOOM)
GO
GO
GO

HAVE YOU SEEN NOPPEKO-CHAN!? SHE WAS LOOKING SO DOWN IN THE DUMPS!!
BUT WHEN WE ASKED AROUND, EVERYONE ELSE WAS JUST AS WORRIED ......
HOW AWFUL!!
A LOT OF FOLKS SURE CARE ABOUT THAT GIRL......

NO WAY! NOT OUR NOPPEKO-CHAN!
NAW, SHE'S A GOOD GIRL.
FOR SURE.

......

AH! SHE'S OPENING THE BOX!
GOSO (RSTL)
GOSO

DON (BAM)
......HMM? WHAT'S THAT? FOOD...?
LOOKS KINDA LIKE A TURKEY......?

SO ALL SHE'S GOT IN THERE IS FOOD......?
THAT MUCH JUST FOR HER BOYFRIEND, THOUGH......?
SHE'S GONE ABOVE AND BEYOND......

THIS DOES FEEL LIKE A LOT FOR A SIMPLE PICNIC DATE......
MAYBE IT'S A SPECIAL DAY FOR THEM?

COME TO THINK OF IT...... IT WAS ABOUT THIS TIME LAST YEAR THAT HER BOYFRIEND SHOWED UP IN ZABO TOWN, RIGHT............?
YEAH, THAT'S WHEN THEY MET AT THE TOWN ENTRANCE.

KAAA (CAW)
KAAA

はあぁぁぁ…

PAAAAA (GLOOOOW)

AND SHE MUST'VE BEEN ALL NERVOUS BECAUSE SHE WAS PREPPING THE SURPRISE...
SOWA (FIDGET)
SOWA
SOWA
DID SHE ASK THE BOYFRIEND TO COME OUT HERE? OH, WHAT A LOVELY SURPRISE. ♪

IS IT ALMOST TIME WHEN THEY'RE S'POSED TO MEET?
!

AND NOW SHE'S OFF TO BRING HIM TO THIS SPOT.
WAKU (EXCITED)
TATA (TROT)
たたっ
THAT BOYFRIEND OF HERS IS IN FOR A SHOCK.
WAKU

OH! HERE THEY COME!
GASA (RUSTLE)

HOW'RE THEY LOOKING?
WELL, HE'S GOT HIS EYES SHUT, AND SHE'S LEADING HIM ALONG.

GUESS THERE WAS NEVER ANY PROBLEM BETWEEN THOSE TWO.
I SUPPOSE WE SHOULD ALL CALL IT A DAY?
SIGH... WE WORRIED OVER NOTHING. THAT'S GOOD ......
HMM? HANG ON.
WHAT'S UP?

BOYFRIEND-SAN OPENED HIS EYES......
!
HUH!? THAT'LL RUIN THE WHOLE SURPRISE, THOUGH!!

T-TELL US WHAT'S GOING ON! DID THE SURPRISE FAIL?
HMM. I'M...... NOT SURE. THEY'RE TALKING NOW......
FROM HIS FACE, IT SEEMS SERIOUS ......
...WHOA!? NOPPEKO-CHAN IS CRYING!?
CRYING!? WHAT!? B-BUT WHY !?
CRYING? REALLY !?
WHAT THE—!? HOW COULD IT ALL GO SO WRONG, JUST LIKE THAT!? WHAT HAPPENED!?
NOT LITERALLY... HARD TO TELL WITH NOPPEKO-CHAN ......
ENOUGH! NOTHING LEFT TO DO...
...BUT ASK THEM TO THEIR FACES!!
DO (SHOVE)
GASA (CRUSTLE)
ACK!? HANG ON, FOLKS!
GASA

DODO (BABAM) どど

WHAT'S GOING ON WITH YOU TWO!?

WH-WHY'RE YOU ALL— OH!
IS THIS SOME KINDA SURPRISE ......?
???

TH-THAT'S RIGHT! NOPPEKO-CHAN SPENT ALL DAY PREPARING FOR THIS!!
YOU WERE A COUPLA STEPS AWAY, BUT YOU MADE HER CRY!
WHAT DID YOU GO AND DO, BOYFRIEND-SAN!?
WAAA (YAP) わー
WAAA わー
わー WAAA

WH-WHAT...... DID I DO ......?

WELL...... I HAD A SURPRISE TOO......

BAKU

BAKU (BABAM)

DOKI (BADUM)

DOKI

DOKI

I SLIPPED IT TO HER WHEN WE HELD HANDS.
?
KORO KORO (ROLL)
KORO KORO
KORO KORO
SU (SHWP)
I HAD NO IDEA YOU ALL WERE HERE AS PART OF HER SURPRISE, THOUGH...... SORRY.

WAIT. SO SHE WAS CRYING WITH JOY?
P-PROBABLY.

W-WE SHOULD BE APOLOGIZING INSTEAD...
SORRY FOR DOUBTING YOU...
??

I DON'T KNOW WHAT FACE YOU'RE MAKING...
!

...BUT CAN I ASSUME IT'S A JOYFUL ONE?

こくり♡
KOKURI (NOD)
"NOPPEKO."
THAT'S WHAT THEY CALL MY GIRLFRIEND, WHO'S GOT NO FACE.
YAAAY!
わあああっ!
CON-GRATS!!

SHE DOESN'T HAVE A VOICE OR FACIAL EXPRESSIONS TO MAKE HER FEELINGS KNOWN, AND YET...

...MORE THAN ANY OTHER, HER FACE IS SHINING BRIGHT...

...AND IS END-LESSLY LOVELY ...

...TO ME.

The GIRL WITHOUT a FACE

Bonus

CHECK IT OUT! SO MANY PEOPLE HAVE SEEN US!
!

AMAZING, RIGHT?
WE'VE NEVER GOTTEN SO MUCH ENGAGE-MENT!
...
JIII (STAAARE) じ——…
...

IT'S GREAT AND ALL, BUT ALSO KINDA EMBAR-RASSING...
JIII じ——…
...

!

WERE YOU EVEN LOOKING AT THE PHONE?
NOPE.

AFTERWORD

THANK YOU SO MUCH FOR PICKING UP *THE GIRL WITHOUT A FACE*! I STARTED PUTTING THIS SERIES ON TWITTER IN MARCH 2019, AND NOW, THANKS TO A LOT OF HELP FROM A LOT OF PEOPLE, I'VE GOTTEN THE CHANCE TO PUT IT OUT LIKE THIS INTO THE WORLD.

TO ALL MY WONDERFUL FOLLOWERS WHO STOOD BY WEEK AFTER WEEK, WITHOUT WHOM A WEB SERIES FROM AN ARTIST LIKE ME SURELY WOULD'VE GONE UNDISCOVERED...
TO MY FRIENDS, WHO STUCK AROUND FOR THOSE LONG PHONE CALLS AND KEPT NUDGING ME FORWARD FROM BEHIND...
TO MY EDITOR, WHO TOOK A CHANCE ON ME...
AND TO YOU, WHO PERHAPS JUST EXPERIENCED MY WORK FOR THE FIRST TIME...
FROM THE BOTTOM OF MY HEART...

THANK YOU!!!

2019.11.10

SPECIAL THANKS!!
TOMU
AONO
MY OTHER TITLE IS BEING SERIALIZED IN COMIC TRAIL TOO! (JAPANESE ONLY)
THANKS !!
TEARON TARON
Twitter:@tearontaron

TRANSLATION NOTES

Common Honorifics
no honorific: Indicates familiarity or closeness; if used without permission or reason, addressing someone in this manner would constitute an insult.
***-san*:** The Japanese equivalent of Mr./Mrs./Miss. If a situation calls for politeness, this is the fail-safe honorific.
***-chan*:** An affectionate honorific indicating familiarity used mostly in reference to girls; also used in reference to cute persons or animals of either gender.
***-sensei*:** A respectful term for teachers, artists, or high-level professionals.

General
Youkai are a class of Japanese supernatural being, translated variously in English as "ghosts," "demons," "monsters," etc. Aside from the boyfriend, all the residents of Zabo Town are *youkai*.

Page 16
Wall-Slam (or *kabedon*) is a common trope in romance manga, where one character has another pinned against a wall. Its name comes from the sound made by a hand slamming against a wall.

Page 51
Noppera-bou are *youkai* who resemble a human being except for one crucial difference: the lack of a face, which they use to frighten people on empty roads late at night.

Page 98
This is a particular kind of Japanese **inn** called a *ryokan*. Common features are meals served to guests, hot baths, and traditional *tatami*-mat flooring.

Page 107
Oobanyaki is a molded griddle cake most commonly filled with sweet red-bean paste, although other fillings exist.

Page 111
Oni are brutish-looking humanoid *youkai* who are typically depicted with horns and large fangs. They are often translated as "ogres."

Page 117
A **toilet-bound girl** spirit with a bob cut named Hanako is a common Japanese urban legend. In some stories, she pulls poor, unsuspecting kids down to hell.

Page 134
Yakisoba is a type of Japanese stir-fried noodles, ***castella*** is a European-inspired Japanese sponge cake, ***soba omelet*** is an omelet filled with *yakisoba*, and ***takoyaki*** are grilled balls of batter filled with octopus meat.

The GIRL WITHOUT a FACE

tearontaron

Translation: CALEB D. COOK
Lettering: BIANCA PISTILLO

Yen Press
150 West 30th Street, 19th Floor
New York, NY 10001

Visit us at yenpress.com
facebook.com/yenpress
twitter.com/yenpress
yenpress.tumblr.com
instagram.com/yenpress

First Yen Press Edition: February 2021

Yen Press is an imprint of Yen Press, LLC.
The Yen Press name and logo are trademarks of Yen Press, LLC.

The publisher is not responsible for websites (or their content) that are not owned by the publisher.

Library of Congress Control Number: 2020950213

ISBNs: 978-1-9753-1987-8 (paperback)
978-1-9753-1988-5 (ebook)

10 9 8 7 6 5 4 3 2 1

WOR

Printed in the United States of